Breakers

Stories from Newfoundland and Labrador

Paul O'Neill

BREAKWATER

*This book is for certain actresses in
the United States of America who
made other times and other places
an enduring memory.*

Andrea Blayne
Evelyn Bohn
Florence Carabee
Teri Duffie
Cloris Leachman
Dolores Marshall
Lillian Stravakis
Muriel Sweep
Louise Williamson

*What their beauty
what their art
never troubled my fond heart.
All I know is
there in line
waits this jostled heart of mine.*

Cover design: *Laurel Angeloff*

Cover Photo: *Michael Messner*

© Copyright Paul O'Neill 1982

Canadian Cataloguing in Publication Data

O'Neill, Paul, 1928-
  Breakers : stories from Newfoundland and Labrador

ISBN 0-919519-22-9 (bound). — ISBN 0-919519-21-0 (pbk.)

1. Newfoundland — History.   2. Labrador — History.
I. Title.

FC2161.053   971.8   C82-095014-9
F1122.053

Foreword

In recounting the attempts to be first to fly the Atlantic, which is included in *Breakers,* Paul O'Neill remarks of Alcock and Brown that had they been Americans "there is no doubt their names will be as well-known in the world today as Charles Lindbergh".

Mr. O'Neill is not only sensitive to the unexploited potential of our history, its events and characters, but has taken steps, with no little success in the medium of this volume, to do something concrete and worthwhile with it. This book puts flesh and blood on the bones of our knowledge of our history. It provides much material which is the stuff of folklore. The "Girl from Fogo" and "Peter Easton" add a new colorful dimension to Fogo and Harbour Grace. The varied choice of events in Newfoundland and Labrador, incorporated into this publication, also provides an insight into the character of the people who have been shaped by them.

The author's style is austere and he is not given to verbiage. He is steeped in history. In his hands, even with the demythologizing, the facts reveal a meaning even deeper and richer than the embellished legends.

Hopefully the contents of this book will be exploited by the modern media of communication and bring them a step closer in becoming part of our tradition.

Mr. O'Neill has rendered another valuable service to us and to Newfoundlanders and Labradorians for generations to come.

Alphonsus L. Penney
Archbishop of St. John's

i

AUTHOR'S NOTE

This work has been prepared for publication in three volumes from articles first written for my column "Around and About" which appeared in the monthly tabloid *The Monitor* from March 1974 to December 1980. There has been some rewriting where necessary to serve the interests of clarity or accuracy. Errors in fact or interpretation are volitional but since time is on the side of truth I will be obliged to future historians to correct any mistakes I may have made when new knowledge and considerations broaden their understanding of things past. I must also apologize to scholars for the frustrating lack of sources but at the time these articles were written their sole purpose was the casual reading pleasure of people with a passing interest in history.

Breakers was made possible by the assistance of a number of people but especially Father Jim Hickey whose idea it was for me to write a monthly column in *The Monitor* when he was its editor, Father Greg Hogan who encouraged my continuing it through difficult and barren periods, and to those whose research resources were ever at my service such as Bobbie Robertson and the Newfoundland Historical Society, Kitty Power and the staff of the Provincial Reference Library, Anne Hart and the staff of the MUN Centre for Newfoundland Studies, and David Davies and the staff of the Provincial Archives of Newfoundland. I am indebted to Archbishop Alphonsus Penney for writing a foreword to this volume.

Contents

Chapter One

Gaspar Corte Real — The Firstcomer

Who is Gaspar Corte Real? Few Newfoundlanders probably know the answer in spite of the fact that a 24 foot high statue of the man, weighing 3½ tons, looms over St. John's, opposite Confederation Building. The Corte Reals are thought to have been an illegitimate branch of the great Portuguese family of Da Costa. They settled on the Algarve and devoted themselves to the service of the Aviz dynasty. Joao Vaz Corte Real was chamberlain to the Infante Don Fernando. He forcibly abducted a Spanish woman in Galicia, married her, and took her with him to the Azores where his rule in the king's name gained him a reputation for cruelty, greed and injustice. When he died in 1496 he left three sons, Vasco, Miguel, and Gaspar. Vasco left the islands and never visited them again, but the two younger brothers remained in the Azores where they were attracted to the maritime life by tales of the sea.

Gaspar Corte Real was born in Portugal around 1450. He is described as "valiant and adventurous and ambitious to win honour." A year after his father's death he moved to the Azores island of Angara where he acted as deputy captain for his brother, Vasco.

In the last days of the 15th century the Azores were filled with Portuguese sailors and they buzzed with talk of new lands to the west. Columbus and Cabot had just completed their voyages of discovery and Portugal was not found wanting when it came to explorers. Vasco da Gama had excited Europe by sailing around Africa to the Indies. Portugal's wealth and empire were on the threshold of greatness.

May 12, 1500, Gaspar received an important patent from King Manuel granting him the privilege "to search out, discover and find...some islands and a mainland." According to the preamble, he had already been on a voyage to the west at his own expense. There is no indication that he found anything on that

1

journey. The "some islands and a mainland" mentioned in the patent probably refers to the discoveries of Christopher Columbus and John Cabot which were still causing considerable excitement. Portugal did not want to be left behind when it came to exploiting new trade routes to China.

No information is available regarding the names or number of ships Corte Real took with him in 1500. He sailed from Lisbon in late spring and at a latitude of about 50^0 North discovered "a land that was very cool with big trees," beyond any doubt it was Newfoundland. He called it Terra Verde. Gaspar was the first to give the island a name. Cabot and Henry VII referred to it merely as the "new land."

It also seems likely that Corte Real discovered and named St. John's on that voyage. There is little likelihood John Cabot ever set eyes on the place. The story of his having sailed into the harbour on St. John's Day is pure myth. The name first appears on Rienel's Portuguese map of 1515 as Rio de San Johem (St. John's River). Fifteen years earlier Gaspar undoubtedly applied the Portuguese name because of the beautiful Waterford River at the upper end of the harbour, then a wide torrent of clear water instead of the sickly stream it is today.

The Corte Real expedition returned to Lisbon in the autumn of 1500. The winter was spent in preparing for another voyage the following spring. Three ships were equipped at Gaspar's own expense and by mid-May he was ready to make a return visit to Newfoundland. There was no way for him to know that Terra Verde was the place already sighted by John Cabot. Full of hope he sailed off with his brother, Miguel, and the blessings of the king.

Two of the ships returned to Lisbon in late autumn, including the one in command of Miguel, carrying a cargo of Indian slaves. They reported that Gaspar had continued to explore southward after sending them home. Instead of Chinese silk King Manuel had to content himself with fifty-seven Beothuck Indians. Alberto Cantino, an Italian diplomat living in Lisbon, reported that the three ships of the argosy had sailed due north for four months without sighting anything and then run into a group of icebergs. A few days later they came upon a field of pack-ice. They then sailed northwest for three months. Cantino's claims are somewhat faulty as the explorers were away for only five months altogether. He states they came at length to a country that was large and delightful, well-watered, covered with pines of mast-tree length, and with "luscious and varied fruits."

In the southern part of the country they captured the fifty-seven natives who were brought back and presented to the king. These aboriginals were probably taken captive in Trinity Bay where the vessels called. The trustful and curious Newfoundland Indians were soon to learn to flee the white man.

A Portuguese observer of the time, Damiano da Gois, writes of the natives the expedition had encountered: "The people in that country are very barbaric and uncivilized, about the same as the natives of Santa Cruz, except that they are white, and they are so affected by the cold that the white color is lost when they grow older, and they then become a good deal darker."

Alberto Cantino wrote: "They live altogether by fishing and hunting animals, in which the land abounds, such as very large deer covered with extremely long hair, the skins of which they use for garments and also make houses and boats there of....Their manner and gestures are most gentle; they laugh considerably and manifest the greatest pleasure....The women have small breasts and the most beautiful bodies, and white attractive faces. The color of their skin must be said to be more white than anything else, while the men are considerably darker." It is interesting to speculate if this whiteness of skin mentioned by both chroniclers owed anything to the Vikings who had settled in Newfoundland 500 years earlier.

Cantino thought the Indians were quite human except for their costumes. He added: "They go quite naked except for their privy parts, which they cover with a skin of the above mentioned deer." The huge, long-haired deer he writes of were probably caribou, an animal unknown to the European explorers. According to Damiano Da Gois, the natives did not hunt with bow and arrow but with "pieces of wood burnt in the fire in place of spears, which, when they throw them, make wounds as if pointed with fine steel....They live in rocky caves and thatched huts."

The Newfoundland Indians were not the first slaves sent from the New World back to Europe. In 1496 Columbus shipped thirty aboriginals to Spain from Hispaniola and in 1500 Ojeda was raiding the Bahamas in search of slaves. However, the Corte Real Newfoundland captives were the first natives from continental North America to be sent into European slavery.

Pasqualigo found evidence in the voyage that "God is with his majesty", and tells us in a letter about Gaspar's explorations that the prospect of obtaining timber for masts and yards "and plenty of men slaves, fit for every kind of labour" was highly pleasing to King Manuel.

If God was with His Majesty he was not with Gaspar himself. His two ships reached Lisbon on the ninth and eleventh of October. Miguel waited in vain for his brother's return. Gaspar was never heard of again. His disappearance on his second voyage to Newfoundland and Labrador was as complete and mysterious as that of John Cabot on his second voyage to the same places.

The following year, when it was obvious Gaspar's ship had been lost with all hands, the king assigned half the territory he thought Gaspar had discovered to Miguel. Not satisfied with this inheritance, Miguel determined to set out in search of his brother. There was a chance that Gaspar had been driven ashore in a storm and survived the northern winter among the laughing natives.

In the spring of 1502 Miguel Corte Real prepared to depart with two well fitted-out vessels. He sailed for Newfoundland in May, but instead of finding some knowledge of his brother's fate, he, too, disappeared. The other ship returned to Lisbon to report that the flagship was lost with all hands. Nothing was ever heard or found of the brothers Corte Real.

By the spring of 1503 when there was no news of Miguel, the oldest of the brothers, Vasco, asked the king's permission to fit-out a fleet and go in search of Gaspar and Miguel. The king, in his wisdom, felt such a search would prove useless and refused permission, probably to the great relief of Vasco. In 1506 King

4

Manuel transferred the missing brothers' rights to Vasco and they remained with his descendents until the family died out some seventy years later. Their claim to Newfoundland ended in 1578 when Manuel Corte Real, the last male of the line, fell in battle fighting the Moors at the side of Don Sebastian, the last Aviz king of Portugal.

Alberto Cantino, the Italian gentleman, had a beautiful world map drawn for Ercole d'Este, Duke of Ferrara, his master. It is still preserved in the Estense Library at Modena. Cantino wanted the map to illustrate all the Portuguese discoveries including those made by Gaspar Corte Real. Chosing to ignore the existence of John Cabot, he planted Portuguese flags on both Newfoundland and Greenland, and stated that the former island was discovered "by command of his most excellent majesty D. Manuel, King of Portugal, by Gaspar Corte Real, a gentleman of the royal household who sent thence a ship with both male and female natives and stayed behind, but never returned...."

One of the most interesting but little known facts about the voyages of Corte Real has to do with a sword Gaspar found in Newfoundland and sent back to Lisbon. According to an observer of the time, "There has been brought hence a piece of broken sword inlaid with gold which we can pronounce to have been made in Italy, and one of the [Indian] children has in his ears two pieces of silver which appear to have certainly been made in Venice — which induces me to believe that the country belonged to the continent." The only rational explanation for the find of the broken sword and Venetian ear-ornaments is that they were left behind, or lost, by some member of John Cabot's party when the famous Venetian explorer went ashore in Newfoundland. That landfall must also have been visited by Corte Real. This indicates a prominent headland such as Cape Bonavista. If, as some historians claim, Cabot's landfall was Cape Breton Island, then Gaspar Corte Real is beyond all doubt the discoverer of Newfoundland. However, if we accept the Cape Breton theory, who, then, was the unknown adventurer who visited Newfoundland before 1500, leaving behind a broken sword and a couple of pieces of silver?

Newfoundland is said to owe a number of its place names to Corte Real. The community which we call Fermeuse he named Formosa, the Portuguese word for "beautiful", unfortunately corrupted by English settlers. Cape Spear is a corruption of Corte Real's Cap da Espero (Cape of Hope) and Cape Race he called Capo Raso (Smooth Cape). He also named Conception and Trinity Bays, and possibly Portugal Cove.

Since it appears Gaspar Corte Real was the first person to discover St. John's harbour he is certainly deserving of the statue of him that stands on Confederation Parkway. The inscription on the base of the statue reads: "Gaspar Corte Real. Portuguese navigator — he reached Terra Nova in the 15th Century — at the beginning of the era of great discoveries. From the Portuguese Fisheries Organization — an expression of gratitude on behalf of the Portuguese Grand Banks Fishermen for the friendly hospitality always extended to them by the people of Terra Nova. May, 1965."

Chapter Two

Bay Bulls — A Chronicle of Then and Now

One of the half dozen oldest communities in Newfoundland is Bay Bulls. The Southern Shore settlement, 18 miles from St. John's, has figured in the history of the island almost from the time of Cabot's discovery. It is the first community on the map of Newfoundland to bear an English name. All the place names on ancient maps, except Bay Bulls, are written in Portuguese, Spanish or French, including St. John's (Rio de San Johem).

The name Bay Bulls first appears in Hood's writings in 1592 as Bay of Bulls. The derivation is a puzzle and may have come from the bull-bird, a common winter resident of Newfoundland occurring in countless numbers on slob ice. Some historians suggest it may have derived from Jersey fishermen who are said to have called it "Buley Bay". Whatever the origin, in all recorded references to the place it is known by its English name.

In 1664, James Yonge, writing in his famous journal, speaks of the community as Bay Bulls, as does Thornton's map of 1689. This shows the settlement to be more than 300 years old. Thornton also records Bread & Cheese Point, another ancient name in the outer harbour.

The first settler at Bay Bulls whose name is known to us is Thomas Cruse, of Ashprington, Devon, who went from London in 1635 to take up residence in the place. It is recorded that "there were not above two or three poor families" living there at the time. Cruse was an independent settler who remained eighteen years and gave evidence hostile to Sir David Kirke in 1667.

According to Cruse's testimony, Sir David, the hero of Quebec, who took over Baltimore's colony and settled at Ferryland in 1639, imposed taxes and collected annual rents on his house besides "a Fate hogg or 10 shillings in law thereof." He accused the Ferryland squire of forcing the inhabitants to take extra land which they did not need, but for which they had to pay rent or be expelled from the island. Cruse also complained that

7

Kirke compelled some of the inhabitants to take out licences for taverns, including himself. It cost him fifteen pounds sterling a year for a licence to operate his tavern at Bay Bulls. The presence of a tippling house in the 1640s shows the community must have had a sizeable transitory population of sailors and fishermen as the "two or three poor families" would hardly make the enterprise pay.

By the 1660s Bay Bulls had become the third largest town in Newfoundland, with ten families. St. John's had fifty families and Harbour Grace was in second place with fifteen. James Yonge, a young English surgeon with the Royal Navy, visited Bay Bulls for the first time in June, 1664. He recorded in his journal, "On Sunday morning we fell within 3 leagues of Cape Despair, the wind northerly. We intended for St. John's but the wind not permitting us we bore away for Bay Bulls, and past by Spout Cove....At noon, we anchored in Bay of Bulls....Here were divers ships fishing....During my stay here I went overland to the next bay, called Witless Bay, 3 mile by land."

In April, 1670, after a fortnight's visit, Yonge reports, "Having stayed in Bay Bulls all this time, living a jolly life, with Mr. Richd. Munyon; Rd. Avent, Caleb Hall and Mr. Hingston, all surgeons of Plymouth and in our mutual carousing spent all our liquor and good things designed for the whole voyage. I had forgotten to mention the smallpox being aboard. Mr. James Cuttiford Junr., Mr. Monk and some others infected, our men also; several had it, but thanks be to God not one died."

By 1726 some sixty-five of the 420 families resident in Newfoundland kept public houses and four of these were at Bay Bulls. The importance of the port is shown in a more positive way by the fact that around 1742, the governor, Admiral Byng, appointed a Deputy Naval Officer for Bay Bulls and vicinity. The man was empowered to act as a preventive officer in the customs service.

The oldest surviving family name would appear to be Stone. The census for 1675 reveals a Jonathan Stone resident in the community. 300 years later there are Stones still living in Bay Bulls. In addition to Stone, in 1675, there was Peter Maye, Jonathan Dale, Robert Pierce and wife, and Jonathan Pierce.

There were two others, probably widows, eleven children and sixty-four servants for a total population of eighty-three persons. There were thirty-five head of cattle, five stages and fifteen boats of which Jonathan Stone owned five.

Another early name which still survives in the community is Hearn. A man named Hearn is said to have escaped from a prison ship at Ferryland in 1734 and settled at Bay Bulls. His crime was probably some infringement of the stringent military regulations, a common offence in those days, but one punished with shocking severity. One deserter in Nova Scotia, taken from Halifax to St. John's, was sentenced to be given 900 lashes on his bare back. He escaped in St. John's, fled north to Trinity, and was not recaptured.

Almost every French attack on St. John's was launched from Bay Bulls. The community has the distinction of having been five times occupied by invading enemy forces, a claim unique in British North America. The first such attack came in the winter of 1696-97 when a force of 120 soldiers from Placentia, under d'Iberville and his brother Bienville, (the founder of New Orleans), marched overland to Ferryland and sailed in small boats to Bay Bulls where the dozen families living in Ferryland had gone to seek refuge. November 21, after only token resistence, Bay Bulls surrendered. The inhabitants and the refugees from Ferryland fled into the woods along with the crew of a 100-ton merchant ship abandoned in the harbour. She was taken by the enemy as a prize. In 1705 with 250 inhabitants of Placentia, 90 regulars and 100 Indians from Nova Scotia under his command, Subercase landed at Bay Bulls at noon, January 26, forced the inhabitants to surrender and plundered considerable provisions. The settlers were taken prisoner and 40 men were assigned to guard them while the French invasion force rested 48 hours before marching to attack St. John's. Fort William surrendered when a settler was scalped by the Indians and sent to the fort as an example of the fate awaiting the defenders if they continued to resist.

The next invasion was in December, 1708, when a French expedition of 164 men, including Indians, attacked Bay Bulls once more while on a march to St. John's. They captured Fort

William almost without a shot being fired after the English went to bed to sleep off a New Year's Eve party. February 2, 1709, the British commander surrendered St. John's to the French commander, St. Ovide, along with the communities of Petty Harbour, Bay Bulls, Quidi Vidi, Torbay, Portugal Cove, and Old Perlican.

June 24, 1762, the inhabitants, fishermen and servants of Bay Bulls saw a squadron of four French ships, under Admiral De Terney, enter their harbour. After a token resistance, the place surrendered and 700 troops under Count d'Haussonville landed and marched on St. John's. They captured the town after a fight and held it until a British force under General Amherst recaptured the island in September, 1763, when Bay Bulls was also "peaceably reoccupied."

The last invasion of any part of British North America by the French was at Bay Bulls in 1796 when 10 ships from Cadiz, under Admiral Richery sailed into the harbour and opened fire on the settlement, after being driven away from St. John's by an English show of might which was actually a bluff mounted by the governor. Among the prisoners carried off from Bay Bulls to Placentia that time was Mr. Justice Dingle, the Magistrate.

Speaking of magistrates it is interesting to note that a trial was held at Bay Bulls as early as September 29, 1680, when Captain Robert Robinson held court on board HMS *Assistance* and tried four of six persons accused of damaging French property at Colinet. The first resident Justice of the Peace at Bay Bulls was a merchant named Nathanial Brooks who was appointed by order of the Governor in 1732.

1817 was a year of near famine conditions in Newfoundland. St. John's was partly destroyed by fire and in the smouldering ruins lay many of the island's winter supplies. Along the Southern Shore the people faced death from starvation. A brigantine, the *Guysborough*, put into Bay Bulls in distress. She was laden with supplies. When it looked as if she would sail again without sharing any of her stores with the hungry populace, a man named John Mulcahey organized the people and led a successful raid on the brigantine. Half her cargo was dispersed among the starving population. A warrant was issued for the arrest of Mulcahey and a reward of twenty pounds sterling offered for his capture. There is no record of his having been taken. He appears to have been a sort of folk hero in the manner of Robin Hood.

In 1931, Dr. Harold Thompson opened a government-owned Fisheries Research Station at Bay Bulls. Its purpose was to attempt to find commercial methods of dealing with fish other than the ordinary salt codfish of commerce. Extensive experiments were carried out. The building was also used to house exhibits from the Newfoundland Museum when it was decided by the Commission that a museum was a luxury Newfoundlanders could ill afford.

April 20, 1937, a portion of the complex leased to the Tors Cove Trading Company was discovered on fire. By midnight the whole place was a mass of flames. No insurance was carried on the building or its contents, including the museum collection. Everything was totally destroyed when the fire truck sent from St. John's got stuck in a snow storm four miles from Bay Bulls.

In the fall of 1974, the Newfoundland and Marine Archaeology Society began underwater excavations on what was then the oldest known wreck in Newfondland waters. She is the 32-gun vessel HMS *Saphire* sunk at Bay Bulls in 1669. The wreck is located near a rivermouth about half a mile east of the church.

The Roman Catholic Church of St. Peter and St. Paul sits atop a knoll at the bottom of the harbour where it overlooked a Royal Canadian Navy dockyard in World War Two. The large wooden edifice was erected in 1890 through the efforts of Rev. Nicholas Roche, the parish priest of the day.

In front of the Church four saints are mounted in the mouths of two large and two small cannon. These statues are said to have been a gift of Sir Michael Cashin who found them in a shipwreck on the Southern Shore. The one-time Prime Minister of Newfoundland was once introduced to a Canadian audience in Quebec as "the only man in North America who canonized four saints."

It must not be thought that Bay Bulls is a relic of history. Today the community plays an important role in the space age.

11

It is the site of the Newfoundland receiver and transmitter for Telesat. At Bay Bulls, television and other microwave signals are received from the space satelites Anik I and Anik II, bringing international radio, television and telephone communications to Newfoundland. The RCA-Bell Canada mast and disc are seen on the right side of the highway as you start down on the St. John's Road into the community.

Chapter Three

The Wreck of the *Anglo-Saxon*

Most of the epics of Newfoundland are calamaties caused by the ruthless ocean, man's carelessness, and uncontrollable winds and tides that have swept vessels, schooners and small fishing boats with their passengers and crews into oblivion. It is impossible in Newfoundland to ignore the great Atlantic Ocean that swirls around its shores. Almost every day it affects the lives of people in many ways.

The sea is a creature of wilful caprice that claims the prudent as well as the careless. There are numerous accounts of ships and people hapless in the fate that brought them to disaster on our coasts. One of the truly pathetic tales is the story of the loss of the SS *Anglo-Saxon*, the most tragic disaster in Newfoundland maritime history.

In April, 1863, the iron-clad steamer sailed from Liverpool for Canada. She stopped at Londonderry, Ireland, to take on a number of immigrant passengers who were by then a lucrative trade. The morning of April 27 dawned bright and clear on the Atlantic. There was a swell but the seas were not rough. The *Anglo-Saxon* ploughed through them at full speed with sails flying from some of her three masts to help the vessel along. When fog and light mist were encountered around breakfast time the sails were taken in and the engines reduced to half speed, about four knots.

The ship was commanded by Captain Burgess, a bearded young Scotsman born in Perth 31 years earlier. He was making his second voyage as master of the *Anglo-Saxon*. On the bridge it was estimated Cape Race was about 17 miles to the northwest. The cannisters of news dispatches from Europe were made ready for dropping overboard to be picked up by the telegraph station on the Cape. In the days before the trans-Atlantic cable, ships from Europe dropped off the latest news in water-tight containers that were fished from the sea and taken to a telegraph station adjoining the Cape Race lighthouse and transmitted to North America several days before the ship could reach an American or Canadian mainland port.

Captain Burgess did not know that the single chronometer on board was faulty and that his ship was actually four miles north of Cape Race, which explains why no soundings were taken. At 11:40 that morning he must have stood frozen in horror as he heard the lookout cry, "Breakers ahead!". A few moments later the Newfoundland coast loomed out of the fog and before any evasive action could be taken to avert disaster, the *Anglo-Saxon* plunged into the cliffs with a shuddering crunch.

As luck would have it the disaster occurred at the only place on that part of the coast where there was any chance of survival. A few hundred feet in either direction and there would probably have been no survivors to tell the tale. Much of the shoreline from Cappahayden to Cape Race consists of steep cliffs that rise a sheer 400 to 500 feet out of the sea. At Clam Cove, where the vessel struck, there was a small river valley where the cliffs dipped down to a ledge of rock about the same height as the sides of an ocean liner of the period.

To the south of the low, wooded cove, there are twin pinnacles of rock and the ship crashed through the breakers between these rocks. The two spires of granite held her firmly by the bow. The jib-boom protruded over the shelf of shore rock and three crew members hastily scrambled ashore with ropes. The great liner twisted to and fro like an animal caught by the nose and trying to free itself from a trap. Anchors were dropped to hold her steady. Fortunately for many, the vise held for about fifteen minutes. During that time most of the steerage passengers who were saved crawled over the jib-boom to land or were pulled to safety in a basket, erected by some sailors as a sort of bosun's chair. First class passengers awaited a more dignified means of going ashore.

Although the rear of the ship was just under water it seems there was no real panic. The huge liner was 283 feet long and 35 feet wide. The 48 cabin (first class) passengers assembled quietly

14

beside the six lifeboats. There was no lifesaving equipment for the 312 steerage passengers which explains why they tried to save themselves as best they could. However, Captain Burgess did urge women and children from steerage to step into any unfilled lifeboats. Only four of the boats got away safely. One was stove in and another was upset as she was being lowered, sending her passengers to their doom in the heavy swell that beat against the shore.

This ceaseless movement of the sea finally smashed the liner against a sunken rock to the south, ending all hope of survival for the ship. Her rudder, screw, and rudder post, were smashed and she swung to the north and was driven side-on against the rocks. At this point many lives might have been saved had the three spars been chopped down and laid across to land as bridges on which to climb ashore. The rail of the doomed vessel was almost level with the shore rocks, but there was a gap of sea in between. For some unexplained reason, no such action was taken. It was thought at first the *Anglo-Saxon* would last many hours, but from the moment she hit the rocks broadside few rescues were accomplished. Panic then began in earnest. Many climbed into the spars only to come crashing down to the decks in a tangle of ropes and cables as the masts broke and fell, crushing those beneath. The single funnel was knocked loose by the sea and rolled over the deck.

Those on land watched helplessly as their relatives and friends screamed for help and scrambled about the rapidly disintegrating wreck. The mess of rigging and splintered masts tossing about in the ocean swell made it impossible for any of the lifeboats to draw near. One had only five persons in it when it reached Cape Race. People were swept from the deck by waves that rolled over it with ease. Many drowned in the tangle of floating debris.

Frightened, cold, wet with rain and April sea water, the survivors huddled in the shelter of the stunted fir trees on shore, watching the horrifying drama unfold. The ship sank lower and lower by the stern until finally she could no longer take the pounding and her decks split wide open. About 60 minutes after striking the rocks, she rolled outwards on her left side and settled fast.

There were no people living in Clam Cove at the time so a party set out on foot for Cape Race, the nearest habitation, four miles to the south. Cappahayden was fourteen miles to the north. There are stories of gallant Newfoundland fishermen being lowered down 500 foot cliffs to rescue some of the passengers. Unfortunately such tales have no basis in fact. There were no cliffs where the *Anglo-Saxon* went ashore and it was three days before a local fisherman appeared on the scene. Eighty-four of the survivors walked over the Imperial Telegraph path to Cape Race. In those days the path was a track four feet wide and in good condition between Cappahayden and the Cape. Twenty-nine others rowed to Cape Race in two lifeboats. Word of the disaster was flashed to St. John's and two ships, the sealer, *Bloodhound,* and the tug, *Dauntless*, were dispatched immediately. The *Bloodhound* went to the Cape where she picked up 113 survivors and took them to St. John's. The *Dauntless* proceeded to Clam Cove next day and saved ten more people, found alive clinging to bits of wreckage in the freezing water.

Of the 446 people on board at the time of the disaster, 209 were saved and 235 lost (erroneously reported in most accounts as 307). Out of 86 crew, 72 were saved, of 48 cabin passengers, 33 were saved, but of 312 steerage passengers, only 104 made it to safety. Sixty-six per cent of the steerage passengers perished and the toll would have been higher, except that many made it to land along the jib-boom and in the basket rigged up by the sailors. The capacity of the *Anglo-Saxon* was 541 passengers. According to the law of the sea at the time, she carried six lifeboats with room for 32 persons in each. Had she been loaded to capacity there would have been no room in these boats for 349 people. As it was, there was no room for 254 and there were no life belts. Amazingly, it was not until after the sinking of the SS *Titanic* in 1912 that these laws were changed.

At St. John's the *Bloodhound,* a vessel which normally carried 90 sealers, was fitted out to hold 200 steerage passengers, and in good spirits despite their tragedy and ordeal, the survivors sailed for Quebec on May 2, after expressing thanks for the overwhelming hospitality shown them by the people of the city. Cabin class passengers left for Halifax the same day on board the SS *Merlin*. Captain Burgess, however, was not among them. The young officer was drowned in the tangle of rigging after the masts broke loose. His body was taken to St. John's and given burial. It is thought he lies in the General Protestant Cemetery on Waterford Bridge Road, but the records of the plots there were lost in a fire, so the grave site is unknown. One hundred of the drowned lie buried at the lonely mouth of Clam Cove Brook.

Two orphans also remained behind, a five-year-old girl, Harriet, and her three-year-old brother, Edward. They did not know their last name. Passengers thought it was Bolton. A grandmother was eventually traced to East London and it was learned the children's name was Walton. They were placed in the Church of England orphanage at St. John's by W.H. Mare. They remained in the orphanage from May 1, 1863, until September 8, 1871. Edward became a draper in the Water Street firm of Philip Hutchings and later emigrated to America. Harriet married a man named Long and became the mother of Joseph Long, who was the father of Hattie Long (Mrs. J.H. Watson) of St. John's. A tea service from the wreck was in her possession until her death in 1981.

In 1871 a fisherman on the southern shore found a wedding ring in the belly of a codfish. It was traced by the Allen Line, owners of the ship, to one of the drowned passengers on the *Anglo-Saxon*, Pauline Burnham, through the unusual engraving, "God above continew our Love". Her relatives in England paid the man £50 ($250) for the keepsake. A meat dish cover from the ill-fated liner is in the possession of the Newfoundland museum on Duckworth Street.

According to Arthur Johnson, the late Newfoundland insurance man who wrote a well-researched unpublished book about the wreck, "The Enquiry says that had not Captain Burgess begrudged the time which would have been taken in sounding for depth of water when approaching the Newfoundland Coast; or if he had slowed to a prudent speed; or had the fog alarm-whistle (proposed since 1861, but scornfully

17

rejected as a "Yankee suggestion") been installed at Cape Race, the dreadful disaster to the almost-new, crack sail-and-propeller, iron liner, *AngloSaxon*, would never have taken place."

Johnson adds that the blame belonged to the captain for trying to make Cape Race as fast as possible. But in this Burgess was only doing what he had to do to hold his job. He did what the captain of every other liner on the Atlantic was doing in a highly competitive traffic. Some companies even offered a penalty for a slow voyage. The enquiry noted of Burgess, "When the fatal accident happened, (he) nobly did his duty and perished in its performance". However, the head of the investigation concluded, "I feel bound...to pronounce that the *Anglo-Saxon* was lost owing to a wrong estimate of the distance run; that there was a culpable omission to use the lead after 8.00 am; and that it is a most reprehensible act on the part of the commander to continue his course in a thick fog, even at half speed, in such an uncertain position."

Captain John Orlebar, who ranks next to Cook as the outstanding surveyor of the Royal Navy, noted, "There are few coasts more safely approachable than the southeastern coast of Newfoundland...if the lead be used and the speed moderate." Orlebar's caution was ignored and the colony witnessed its greatest sea disaster at Clam Cove, April 27, 1863.

Chapter Four

Newfoundland's Dog in Fact and Fiction

In all of Canada, the only purebred dogs native to the country are the Nova Scotia Retriever (or Duck Tolling Dog), the Labrador Retriever and its close relative, the Newfoundland. For a century, people have speculated on the origin of the Newfoundland dog. For a long time, it was believed to have descended from the Pyrenean mountain dog, crossed with a spaniel from the northern part of Spain, or with an English sporting dog. Now that L'Anse aux Meadows in northern Newfoundland has conclusively proven to be a Viking settlement, probably Leif Ericsson's Vinland colony, the origin of the dog has been established with a greater degree of authority. We know from the Norse sagas that Ericsson and the Vikings brought with them to Vinland shortly before the year 1000 A.D. the large black "Bear Dog." In Norway these dogs were used as beasts of burden for hauling and also as guardians. Most probably they derived from the Tibetan Mastiff. The Bear Dog of the Norse was undoubtedly left behind when the Vikings departed Newfoundland. Some had probably run wild and it is thought they mated with the local Indian water dog. While left undisturbed for over 500 years the two breeds developed into one dog that survived by adapting to the cold and the water, since it frequently had to swim to get from one point of land to another.

Following the rediscovery of Newfoundland by John Cabot in 1497, the Spanish fishermen who came to the island brought with them the beautiful Great Pyrenese dog of the Basques, and it was then that the Pyrenean mountain dog may have played a part in the further development of the Newfoundland breed. A parti-coloured dog was evolved in England, but all-black became the dominant colour.

Early explorers coming to Newfoundland reported seeing a

large black water-dog wandering with the native Indians. Captain George Cartwright is credited with naming the dog after the island around 1775 when he was exploring the coasts of Labrador.

In 1780, Governor Edwards decided to encourage sheep raising in the colony. To cut down on the menace to the sheep, he decreed that there should not be ownership of more than one dog per family. For most breeds this did not matter as they existed in abundance elsewhere in the world. For the Newfoundland dog it almost meant extinction of the breed, since few existed outside the island. Their numbers dwindled considerably, but sheep raising never caught on and the breed gradually recovered until the beginning of the present century, when it was reckoned there were about 2000 Newfoundlands on the island. Once more legislation was introduced to protect flocks of sheep that the government of the day imagined would whiten the hills of Avalon. The breed again faced extinction. What dogs there were became mongrelized.

Mr. Harold Macpherson of Westerland Farm in St. John's is credited with having saved the Newfoundland dog from oblivion. As early as 1766, Sir Joseph Banks came to the island in the hope of procuring for himself a Newfoundland dog. However, he reported in his journal, "Those I met with were mostly Curs with a Cross of the Mastiff in them."

The Newfoundland is a superb example of Darwin's theory of "survival of the fittest." In the 700 years from the departure of the Vikings from the northern part of the island, to the arrival of such men as Cartwright and Banks in the eighteenth century, the dog had developed unique life-saving characteristics and an ability to survive the freezing Atlantic Ocean because of a waterproof double coat. The web feet were another aid to its survival. Roaming the hills with their Indian and Inuit owners, the dogs developed a deep affection for man as they were welcomed in the Indian mamteeks for their warmth and rarely, if ever, mistreated.

There are many interesting stories told about Newfoundland dogs, including several popular myths. Perhaps the most often told myth is the one which claims that Lord

Byron's dog, Boatswain, was a Newfoundland. In order to track down that story, I visited the ruins of Byron's home, Newstead Abbey, in England. In a show of pagan defiance, the young poet buried Boatswain on the site of the abbey altar. With him was interred Joe Murray, a manservant. It was Byron's intention that he himself and another manservant, William Fletcher, would also be buried with the dog, but scandal forced him to flee England and he died abroad.

The inscription on Boatswain's tomb ends with the words "...a just tribute to the memory of Boatswain, a dog who was born at Newfoundland May 1803 and died at Newstead Abbey November 18, 1808." It makes no other claim. On careful examination it will be seen that the wording says only that the dog was born at Newfoundland. An oil painting, which I was shown upstairs in the Abbey, and done from life, shows Boatswain as a knee high animal with a pointed snout, bushy tail and white ruff on his neck. He appears to be a sheep dog or border collie. Sheep dogs were not uncommon in Newfoundland in the early 1800s, but how one found his way to Lord Byron is unknown. All we can be sure of is that Boatswain was not a Newfoundland.

Another popular myth tells how a Newfoundland dog saved the passengers and crew of the SS *Ethie* when that steamer ran ashore at Martin's point, Bonne Bay, December 11, 1919. One legend has the lifeboats washed away and pounding surf preventing the men on shore from launching a rescue boat. The last hope of those on board lay with the ship's Newfoundland dog, Tang, making it to shore. The captain ordered Tang overboard and the animal leaped into the foam with an end of rope in his mouth. When he reached land, a boatswain's chair was rigged with the rope and all on board the stricken vessel were saved. The story had Tang being given a Meritorious Service medal from Lloyds of London which he is said to have worn on his collar until he died in St. John's of old age. Another version has the big Newfoundland belonging to a fisherman on shore and swimming out from the beach, grabbing the rope in his teeth and carrying it to shore.

The facts of the tale, as I gathered them from a survivor of the wreck, now a clergyman's wife, and from author Cassie Brown, who investigated the case, show that the dog was a frisky mongrel who belonged to an old fisherman on shore. As the men floundered about in the surf trying to catch the rope thrown from the ship, the playful mastiff caught the end of it in his mouth and pulled with the fishermen. An American reporter exaggerated the incident to improve his story. The dog, afterwards named "Hero", was actually given an award by a humane society in Philadelphia. Whatever the merits of the award he was not a Newfoundland dog.

Richard Wagner, the German composer, once introduced his two Newfoundlands at a dinner party, saying "We shall now be entertained by nature's gentlemen." Robert Burns, the Scottish poet, wrote of Caesar, his Newfoundland dog, that he was a gentleman and a scholar and "though he was o' high degree, the fient a pride — nae pride had he." Senator Robert Kennedy, Humphrey Bogart and other celebrities have been owners of the breed.

One of the greatest boosters of the Newfoundland dog during the last century was Eliza Gilbert, Irish born daughter of Lady Craigie, but better known to the world as the tempestuous actress-dancer, Lola Montez. At the age of twenty-nine Lola arrived in Munich, where she captivated the heart of King Ludwig 1. Already she had been known as the mistress of Franz Liszt and Alexandre Dumas (pere). An intimate of George Sand, she was also an acquaintance of Palmerston and Disraeli. Fearful of her progressive reforms as uncrowned queen of Bavaria, Prince Metternich, who was Lola's implacable enemy, eventually helped oust her and her flight in 1848 led to the abdication of the king. She fled Bavaria with a box of jewels and the title of Countess of Landsfeld.

Her grand tour of the United States as actress-dancer brought her to San Francisco in the gold rush and she settled for some years in nearby Grass Valley. Eventually Lola went on the lecture circuit telling of her exploits. The last of the great courtesans finally got religion and ended her days saving fallen women in New York, where she died sick and almost penniless January 17, 1861, at the age of forty-three.

On a lovely May day in 1849, as the provocative Lola walked in London's Hyde Park, a handsome young man who was a coronet in the second regiment of the Life Guards drove by in his carriage with a huge Newfoundland dog sitting beside him. Lola, who loved animals, was impressed and found out he was George Trafford Heald. In the days that followed, whenever she walked in the park, she was conscious of him admiring her fiery beauty as he drove past. Through a friend she found out he wished to sell the dog and, wanting to own the huge Newfoundland, she invited Lieutenant Heald to her residence. By July 19, two months after their meeting in the park, they were married. Through a misunderstanding about divorce arrangements, Lola married Heald while she still had a husband serving with the British Army in India. She was forced to flee to the continent to avoid arrest on a bigamy charge. According to the *New York Herald*, October 10, 1849, she landed at Boulogne with the large black Newfoundland dog and headed for the Hotel de Londres, where she shared a suite with the animal. When Heald later joined her, they could be seen strolling around the port or walking along the seafront with the dog.

After her marriage to Heald collapsed, Lola went on to other turbulent affairs and adventures, but she was seldom ever without her Newfoundland dog. Whether or not it was the same dog, it is impossible to say.

In the autumn of 1858, Lola decided to take her lectures to Ireland and England. On November 8, she sailed from New York on board the North American Line steamer, *Pacific*. On the thirteenth the ship reached St. John's,. where it docked overnight, and Lola Montez saw for herself the country that had given her beloved dog to the world. There was undoubtedly great excitement along Water Street when the identity of the passenger from the steamer became known. Having coaled, the *Pacific* sailed next day for Galway, taking among its Newfoundland passengers Frederic Gisborne, off to Britain on the business of his Atlantic telegraph, and such socially prominent ladies as Mrs. W. H. Mare, Mrs. David Rennie, and Mrs. Hugh Hoyles, the wife of the future Prime Minister.

In the summer of 1859 Lola was reported wandering about London, muttering to herself and reading the Bible to anyone who would listen. Her final religious mania had begun. She was seen sitting in Regent's Park, a tired figure in black, reading the New Testament with a big Newfoundland dog beside her. When a reporter asked her if she were Lola Montez she answered, "Who I am is no matter." The man reported that some children fled from her dog, but she lured them back by showing how harmless he was. Lola took a large house in Park Lane for herself and the dog, but became totally disorganized and had a nervous breakdown. Two years later she was dead. The fate of her Newfoundland is unknown. King Ludwig died in Nice seven years after Lola, swearing on his death bed that she had never been his mistress, but that theirs had been an innocent love that had "held joys second to none."

Without the Newfoundland dog there would probably have been no battle of Waterloo and no great hero called Wellington. One dark night in February, 1815, as the Emperor Napoleon's captors dined, danced and celebrated at the Congress of Vienna, the idol of France slipped and fell into the murky waters as he was attempting to escape prison on the island of Elba. The sailors who were assisting in the escape could not find him in the darkness and the emperor, who was unable to swim, began to drown. Just when all seemed lost, a Newfoundland dog in one of the boats leaped into the water, found Napoleon, and swam with him to safety so that, once more, France was able to rally to its immortal leader for the hundred days that ended disastrously at Waterloo.

Those who have read or seen performed Sir James Barrie's immortal *Peter Pan* will know that the Darling children had a large black and white Newfoundland dog named Nana who appears on stage in the work. Nana is what is known as a Landseer. This black and white Newfoundland was evolved sometime between 1550 and 1700 by mating the all-black Newfoundland with the white Estate dogs of England. It took two hundred years of cross-breeding to standardize the type which was immortalized by the popular Victorian artist, Sir Edwin Landseer, in his painting, "A Distinguished Member of the Humane Society." The breed was legitimized with the name "Landseer." While it is a Newfoundland, it is not the true and original native dog of the island.

A close look at other dogs reveals that several breeds have the Newfoundland as a main ancestor. The Labrador Retriever, originally known as the St. John's dog, is a very close relation. The name Labrador was given the dog for show purposes in England, where it sounded more exotic than St. John's. The Chesapeake Retriever evolved from two Newfoundland dogs, Canton and Sailor (shipwrecked on both sides of Chesapeak Bay). As they grew up they mated with the local hunting dogs until, finally, offspring from both sides of the Bay were united in a distinct breed. Two important German dogs, the Leonberger and the Bernhardiner, are also partly descended from the Newfoundland.

While its size makes it one of the largest breeds of dog in the world, the Newfoundland is among the most trustworthy and kindest of animals. Its great lifesaving ability in the water is well known, as is its gentleness, affection and devotion. Its beauty and dignity give it a special place in all our hearts.

Chapter Five

Bishop Feild And His Masterpiece Cathedral

In 1758, nearly sixty years after the appointment of the first Church of England clergyman to St. John's, the Rev. Edward Langham erected the first proper church on a piece of land where the gallows formerly stood, opposite the court house on the Upper Path (Duckworth Street). Early in 1800 work was begun on the construction of a new church above this old chapel. It was occupied on October 19th, but not consecrated until the visit to St. John's by Bishop John Inglis of Nova Scotia in 1827. It was an almost square building twenty-one feet high. The bishop described the parish church as "a spacious and respectable wooden building, commodious and in good repair." King George had contributed 200 guineas to its construction.

The Diocese of Newfoundland was founded in 1839 with the Venerable Aubrey George Spencer as first bishop. Born at Mayfair in 1795 he was a grandson of the second Duke of Marlborough and is an ancestor of both Sir Winston Spencer Churchill and Lady Diana Spencer, who in the summer of 1981, became England's future queen by her marriage to Charles, Prince of Wales.

In 1840 the new bishop wrote that "the condition of the church was indeed so deplorable as to divest the service of religion of much of the veneration and dignity which rightly belongs to it." He was also impressed "with a mournful sense of the small proportion of our worldly substance which had been bestowed on the sanctuary of God." He addressed a Pastoral Letter to the people of the diocese asking for funds to build a cathedral. He sent Rev. T.F.H. Bridge to England with the same appeal.

Sir John Harvey, Governor of Newfoundland, whose son married the Bishop's daughter, gave a hundred pounds to which Dr. Spencer added a hundred pounds of his own, urging the faithful not to be distracted "from consecrating your exertions in

26

the holy cause of transmitting an enlarged and improved sanctuary to your descendants." In one day he collected £1430 from eighteen subscribers.

Animosities arose over the site of the proposed cathedral. The Bishop put an end to them by himself deciding that the best place was the existing churchyard "with due care to the rights of those who have an interest in the graves." The churchyard was still the major burial ground in St. John's and it contained such noted corpses as Lady Kirke, Dr. William Carson and Rev. John Jones. The plans were drawn locally by James Purcell at a cost of twenty pounds. The Irish architect had been brought from Cork to superintend the building of the Roman Catholic Cathedral. May 18, 1843, some eighteen hundred tons of cut limestone were shipped to St. John's for use in building the Church of England Cathedral which was to be 120 feet long, 56 feet wide, and with a spire 130 feet high. A drawing of this church appears in Philip Tocque's *Wandering Thoughts* as the "Church of England Cathedral, St. John's."

August 21, 1843, four days before he was to leave Newfoundland for his new See of Jamaica, Dr. Spencer laid the foundation stone of the cathedral. Governor Harvey attended the ceremony and gave an address. The proposed cost had escalated from the Bishop's original estimate of four thousand pounds to seven thousand pounds. In spite of the laying of the cornerstone, work on the foundation was never begun and the stone itself disappeared from history. The new Bishop of Newfoundland, Edward Feild, had other priorities. A rigorous and ascetic man, accused by his opponents of a love of autocratic power, he was much more interested in the establishment and endowment of a theological college at St. John's than in building a cathedral. The provision of adequate buildings for what he called Queen's College was one of the first things to engage his attention. He bought a piece of land on Forest Road "with a neat cottage upon it" to which he added a hall and dormitories for the students.

Dr. Spencer's scheme to erect a cathedral "worthy to be the metropolitan church of an extensive see" would have belonged to the distant future, except that the hand of fate made it much

27

more immediate. June 9, 1846, a pot of glue in the shop of Hamlin, the cabinet maker, on the corner of George and Queen Streets, boiled over around 8:30 in the morning, starting a fire that by sundown had destroyed two thirds of the city, including the Church of England house of worship on Gower Street, at Church Hill. The Cork limestone, stored in weatherbeaten crates on the site, cracked and broke into useless pieces when the wooden crates burned.

Bishop Feild was left without a choice. He would now have to divert funds to the building of a cathedral. June 12, 1846, he wrote to a friend: "Little did I think when on Sunday last I ordained two priests and eight deacons in our old church, and complained that such a structure, so mean and miserable, was ill adapted to the sacred service, that I should never officiate again there, and that in two days not a vestige of the building would remain, and I should wish in vain for half the accommodation I perhaps too lightly esteemed."

The bishop was urged by the clergy and laity to visit England to relieve the lot of the fire sufferers who had lost everything and secure substantial aid to build a new church. He set out on board the church ship *Hawk* with an invalid clergyman, a theological student, and two other persons who wanted passage. In spite of a hurricane which "strewed the Atlantic with wreck" he landed at the Devonshire port of Torbay on October 6, having lost mainsail, gaff, topmast and stay-sail. The *Hawk*'s bulwarks were started in several places and other damage done.

January 9, 1847, Dr. Feild arrived back in St. John's, via Halifax, to find the people of the fire-devastated city suffering through an exceptionally severe winter. On arrival the thermometer was considerably below zero and a sharp wind was blowing offshore. The steamer, covered in ice, was unable to enter port and he was taken to land in a small boat with great difficulty. In the bishop's own drawing-room the temperature fell to 3°F below zero, and the water froze on the table while he was dining. When he laid down that night to rest from his journey he found "getting into bed is something like plunging into a cold bath." He was awakened by the discharge of two guns from the fort to find the fashionable house of a neighbour, Captain Spearman, the Collector of Customs, enveloped in flames. The Collegiate School and the students' house were being showered by burning flakes and embers, but were saved because the water poured on the roofs instantly became ice, protecting the wooden shingles.

Bishop Feild had collected an impressive sum of money in the churches of England on the authority of the Queen's Letter. He stated that the building of a cathedral would be one of the objects on which part of the money would be spent. The statement was to plunge him into the kind of misunderstanding with other denominations that was to plague him throughout his episcopacy. It was claimed that the money should be distributed equally to fire sufferers. That which had been contributed in England was given by English churchmen, but the majority of those burned out in St. John's were Roman Catholics. By giving them only a small portion of what he had collected the bishop was accused of diverting relief money to his own purposes. He wrote to a friend of these problems: "If you knew half the grief and anxiety I suffer about it, — but I forbear."

While in England Bishop Feild had scrapped the plans drawn by Purcell for Dr. Spencer's cathedral and come up with a grandiose design by a leading proponent of the Gothic Revival in England, Sir George Gilbert Scott. On his travels throughout the country his appeal fell on the ears of the famous architect to whom he was introduced and on his return to St. John's he carried in his portmanteau Scott's plans for one of the finest neo-gothic churches in North America.

While preparations went ahead for the opening up of ground for the new foundations, Bishop Feild worried about the church ship, *Hawk*. She had sailed from Torquay on April 18 and was overdue. There had been a hurricane on the Atlantic and many ships were lost. The bishop wrote: "My hand shakes and my heart quakes....Could I remain here, if she should be lost with all her precious cargo?" Then on May 25, the day the ground was to be opened, the wounded vessel limped into St. John's harbour, "her cargo safe and sound, for the little bird herself had been sadly beaten and battered."

The Bishop went on board and welcomed the passengers and crew with his episcopal blessing. At the Central School he held a service at which Holy Communion was administered to them all. After that work was begun on digging out the foundations. "I had as many as fifty men giving voluntary labour, and, I trust, shall have nearly as many men every day this week." Dr. Feild worried that the cost of the nave alone would be £15,000 in England, or £25,000 in Newfoundland. He agonized: "This appears to me Mid-summer madness. Even if we had the money, would it be right to spend such an enormous sum on the material temple, while bodies and souls are starving for the lack of necessary food. S. Wulstun is said to have wept when he saw the great pile of his cathedral going up, because, he said, they had left building temples of men to build one of stones." These thoughts are a little paradoxical, for it was Feild himself who scrapped the modest cathedral designed by Purcell for the grand scheme of Sir George Gilbert Scott.

The structure was to be 188 feet long, 99 feet wide and 80 feet high to the ridge of the roof which was to be vaulted with a tower and spire. Twelve thousand tons of cut stone were ordered from England and Ireland to replace that lost in the 1846 fire and flagstone for the roof was ordered from France. The work of preparing the foundation was carried on into the winter of 1847-48 until frost and snow compelled the builders to give up. The walls were carefully covered to shelter them from the weather until work could be resumed in the spring.

In spite of financial problems, Bishop Feild was able to open the completed nave to worship on September 21, 1850. Thirty years were to pass before construction on the rest of the cathedral was resumed. It was St. Matthew's Day and the ceremony of consecration was followed by the first general Ordination. All seats were free because the bishop felt he owed it to the character of the building and the friends in England who had supplied funds. He thought that if the only difference between a church and a cathedral was the presence of a bishop's chair then that would have to suffice, for his own could afford none of the usual important properties of a cathedral such as the Dean and Chapter, Choir, etc. Christmas Day, 1851, the vessels, book and pastoral staff presented by anonymous friends in England to the cathedral, were solemnly consecrated by the bishop. After that he turned his attention away from building to other matters, as he found he was embroiled in a wrangle with dissenting Protestants over obtaining a separate share of the grant made by the government for educational purposes. He declined to allow his faith to be ranked as one of the Protestant sects. Although it exposed him to personal vilification, the bishop's stand resulted in the denominational system of education which exists in Newfoundland today.

At a meeting on January 5, 1880, Bishop Jones remarked: "Outside Bishop Feild's work in the diocese there was no memorial in the colony to testify to the manner in which the Church had appreciated his life and labours," and suggested there could be no more fitting memorial than the completion of the cathedral "which Bishop Feild had begun on so grand a scale." Dr. Jones's suggestion was acted on with great enthusiasm and within five years the choir and transepts were built and consecrated. All that remained was the addition of the tower and spire.

July 8, 1892, it was 87°F in St. John's. Late in the afternoon, a drayman named Fitzpatrick dropped a lighted pipe of tobacco, catching fire to some hay in the barn of his employer, Timothy O'Brien. By dawn the following morning half the city of St. John's lay in smouldering ruins. One of the victims of the "Great Fire of 1892" was the recently completed Cathedral of St. John the Baptist. As the flames swept down Long's Hill towards the ediface, Bishop Jones stored documents and other valuables in the crypt of the church. A policeman stood guard at the door to make sure no spark entered the building. However, the intense heat melted the panes of lead around the glass of the windows and fire got inside that way. Shortly after seven o'clock in the evening the oak rafters ignited under the slate roof and the neo-Gothic masterpiece tumbled into the flames which leaped hundreds of feet into the air as the moulded arches and massive pillars crumbled, causing the loft roof to fall in.

In an address to the Synod in 1902, Bishop Jones urged reconstruction of the Cathedral. On June 24, after a brief service held by the bishop amidst the ruins, work was commenced on clearing away the immense mass of debris. This was done by free labour. By July 18, it was finished. Men and boys, Anglicans, dissenting Protestants and Roman Catholics laboured into the night, week after week, when their regular working hours were over, to get the job done. The Star of the Sea Society, a Roman Catholic organization, played a football match that raised $400 towards expenses.

The rebuilt nave was blessed September 21, 1905, in the presence of the rector of St. James's Church, New York, a former bishop of Nova Scotia. The completion of the tower and spire was urged that year, but had to be postponed due to lack of funds. They remain uncompleted for the same reason. Since 1955, considerable sums of money have been poured into reconstruction and replacement of much of the stone damaged in the fire of 1892. As this work eats up inflated dollars, the roof of the Nave and Choir are also unfinished. At this point it is doubtful that the masterpiece of Sir George Gilbert Scott will ever see completion.

Chapter Six

Ann Harvey — Newfoundland's Grace Darling

In the summer of 1975, I found myself in the parish churchyard of the little English village of Bamburgh on the north east coast of Northumberland. The tombstone in front of me was inscribed with the name GRACE HORSLEY DARLING. Across the roadway was the house in which Grace Darling was born on November 24, 1815, and next to the house stood the Grace Darling Museum opened in 1938 by the ninth Duke of Northumberland on the centenary of the event which made the lighthouse keeper's daughter famous in English history.

At the time of her birth in Bamburgh, Grace's father was light-keeper on Brownsman Island, a desolate place devoid of everything but coarse grass and sea birds. She was taken there for the first time in December 1815. It was her home for the next eleven years, at which time her father was appointed to the new Longstone Light on the outermost of the Farne Islands. There she learned to live with hurricanes and severe gales as constant companions. Even though she was one of nine children, life on the islands was as lonely for the little girl as it was hazardous and uncomfortable.

Grace was taught to read and write by her parents, and to knit, spin and sew. By the time she was nineteen, all the family had left the lighthouse for life on the mainland, with the exception of Grace and her younger brother, William Brooks, who remained with their father. On September 7, 1838, when she was 22 years of age, fate wrote Grace Darling's name into history. At about 4:00 a.m. the paddle steamship, *Forfarshire*, on a passage from Hull to Dundee, struck Big Harcar in the Farne Islands and almost at once broke in two. A luxury liner of her time, she carried 400 tons of freight and 61 or 63 passengers; reports vary. The captain, Mr. Humble, had his wife with him and neither survived the wreck.

On the passage from England to Scotland, a leak in the engine caused the steam to fail and north of the Tweed the engines stopped. Captain Humble made sail to try to reach the Inner Farne Island, but he misjudged his course in the tremendous seas and gale force winds. The *Forfarshire* struck Big Harcar, a tiny island, three or four hundred yards from Longstone Light. At a quarter to five, Grace looked out from her bedroom window and saw the stricken ship, but because it was not yet daylight and the seas rolling over the wreck, she could see no sign of life. She watched incessantly with a spy glass until nearly seven o'clock. That was when the first movement of survivors was seen on the reef. She immediately informed her father.

William Darling and his daughter launched their boat, a four-oared cobble measuring 21½ feet from stem to stern, and 5 ft. 4 in. amidships. Since William Brooks was on the mainland visiting friends in Seahouses, Grace offered to aid her father in the rescue. Braving the high seas, they reached the reef to find nine persons alive on it. It was impossible to accommodate them all in the cobble. They took five that first trip, including a woman. William Darling returned with two crew members for the rest of the survivors. A lifeboat had been lowered and was found to be miraculously preserved with nine more people on board. Darling reported 43 persons drowned in the wreck.

Within weeks of the rescue Grace Darling became a national heroine. On September 14, the Newcastle *Courant* told her story to the world and painted a glowing picture of her role in the rescue, but it was the Newcastle *Journal* of the following day that suggested she had taken the initiative in the tragedy and "with matchless intrepidity seized the oar and entered the boat". Other newspapers around the world carried the account. A stream of curious visitors descended on the Farne Islands, hopeful for a glimpse of Grace. The poet, Wordsworth, called her "A guardian spirit sent from pitying heaven, In Woman's shape". It was felt the girl should be rewarded for her deed and a subscription was opened. Queen Victoria herself contributed fifty pounds. The Royal National Institute for the Preservation of Life from Shipwreck awarded silver medals to William

Darling and his daughter. The Royal Humane Society gave them each a gold medallion. Grace received a silver medal from the Glasgow Humane Society.

The honours might have continued to come except that the young heroine's health began to decline in 1841. She moved to the mainland where she was attended by the Duchess of Northumberland's own physician. October 20, 1842, she died of tuberculosis at the age of twenty-six in the house of her sister in Bamburgh, now a Grace Darling curio shop, and was buried in the parish churchyard. At the height of the excitement caused by her deed, the staid London *Times* was moved to ask: ..."Is there in the whole field of history, or of fiction even, one instance of female heroism to compare for one moment with this?" The answer was "Yes", but she was living far away in Newfoundland. Her name was Ann Harvey. In time she was to be tagged by local writers and historians with the soubriquet..."The Grace Darling of Newfoundland".

There are several coincidences between the life of Grace Darling and that of Ann Harvey. Both girls were born to large families in the year 1815, and each lived at home with her parents and a younger brother on an isolated sea coast. George Harvey, Ann's father, was a fisherman who lived at Isle aux Morts, near Port aux Basques. The French settlers in Newfoundland had named the community Isle of Death, because of the large number of ships and voyagers who met their doom on the nearby coast, many of them passengers bound to or from Canada. George Harvey had risked his life a number of times to save these unfortunates.

July 12, 1828, ten years before Grace Darling was to electrify the world by her act of courage, the brigantine *Dispatch*, bound from Londonderry, Ireland, to Quebec, in Lower Canada, drove ashore on Wreck Rock (as it afterwards became known) near Isle aux Morts. The weather that year was rough and stormy and the vessel with her 163 passengers and crew ran into a tremendous gale as she attempted to round the southwest tip of Newfoundland. Driven on land by the force of the wind, she struck the rocks about three miles from the Harvey home.

There was no way for those on the brig to reach the safety of the shore, so they began to send up rockets and other distress signals. Some accounts state that George Harvey heard or saw these signals and with his seventeen-year-old daughter, Ann, and his twelve-year-old son, Tom, went to the rescue in his open boat. Another account has Harvey, Ann and Tom out in their punt with their dog when they saw six men on a beach. On investigation they turned out to be survivors of the *Dispatch*.

Because of the gale of wind that was blowing, it seems more probable that one of the Harveys spotted the flares and the father, daughter and son launched their small boat in the storm-tossed seas and rowed against the howling wind to the doomed ship. Ann and her brother, with their father, manned the oars, giving no thought to their own safety.

Due to the fierceness of the sea, it was impossible to go near the wrecked vessel to rescue the passengers and crew huddled in the area of the forecastle. Legend has it that Harvey sent his dog overboard and the animal swam to the vessel where eager hands grabbed it and tied a light line to its neck. The dog then swam back to its master's small boat and was hauled aboard by Ann and her father. The trio then rowed with the line to land.

Whatever the truth of the matter, a line from the foundering ship was used to haul a stout rope to shore which Harvey and his daughter secured to make possible a breeches-buoy. Six men were brought to safety. Harvey took four of them with him and directed positioning of three boats which saved sixty more people. According to one fairly reliable account, the storm made it impossible to save the rest of the survivors that day. Thirty were got off the second day and the remainder the day after. Another account has all 163 persons saved the first day by the breeches-buoy. A number of bodies are said to have been washed into Burnt Island Harbour where they were taken from the water by Benjamin Keeping, the first settler there.

Regardless of how long it took to get the survivors to shore, George Harvey had to keep the shipwrecked people in Isle aux Morts for two weeks, waiting for the seas to abate. Some stayed in his house and others in makeshift shelters. We are told that ten died soon after reaching land. These may have been the bodies that washed ashore at Burnt Island Harbour. It was no easy job for George Harvey and Ann (there is no mention anywhere of a Mrs. Harvey) to cope with feeding so many people from their meagre supply of flour, tea and salt fish. Harvey is supposed to have carried a heavy cane with him, and if a survivor at the table reached for more than his allotted share of food, the host did not hesitate to use the stick on the offending hand.

After about two weeks, George Harvey was able to take some of the ship-wrecked in his boat to Port aux Basques. Three weeks after the mishap a rescue vessel arrived from La Poile. The remainder of the survivors were then taken from La Poile to St. John's on board the British warship HMS *Tyne* commanded by Sir Richard Grant.

It was Sir Richard who acquainted Governor Cochrane with the part played in the amazing rescue by George, Ann and Tom Harvey. Cochrane got in touch with the British Government and a special gold medal was struck to commemorate the event. Harvey was rewarded with one hundred pounds from a subscriber of Lloyd's. The medal was taken to Isle aux Morts by Governor Cochrane but the Harveys were away at the time of His Excellency's visit. It was passed to Archdeacon Wix who finally presented it to Ann Harvey after a church service, when he visited Isle Aux Morts September 29, 1830.

The inscription on the medal read: "...Presented to George Harvey in token of the sense entertained by His Majesty's Government of his humane exertions in preserving the lives of the passengers and crew of the brig *Dispatch* wrecked near Dead Island on the coast of Newfoundland 10th July, 1828"Queen Victoria is said to have sent a letter in her own handwriting praising the heroism of George Harvey, his daughter, Ann, and young son, Tom. A search was made for the medal by relatives in later years but it was never found.

Canon H.W. Cunningham, D.D., who edited the notes of his brother-in-law, Joseph H. Small, for many years the Stipendiary Magistrate of Burgeo, found in Small's notes how it was recorded in London that Mr. Newman of Newman and Company wished to obtain Harvey's dog and wrote him to the effect asking him to name his price for the animal. Cunningham reports Harvey's reply as follows: "Mr. Newman I understands you wants to buy the 'Hairy Man'. His tail's cut short, ears close to his head. The price of my dog is a hundred of bread". It is not recorded if Newman took up the fisherman's offer.

September 14, 1838, just one week after Grace Darling's heroic actions in England, George and Ann Harvey saved the lives of twenty-five members of the crew of the Glasgow ship *Rankin,* with Alexander Mitchell as master, when she ran on the rocks at Isle aux Morts. According to an account by John B. Jukes, Newfoundland's first geological surveyor, Ann Harvey again took part in this rescue. A number of trips were made to the stricken vessel until all on board were saved. Jukes visited Isle aux Morts in 1839 and reported that Harvey had not received any payment for the food, clothing and shelter he gave the castaways of either wreck.

Ann Harvey's fate was kinder than that of her more famous contemporary, Grace Darling, for she married and became Mrs. Charles Gillam. However, there is nothing in the Port aux Basques-Isle aux Morts area to commemorate the heroism of this brave Newfoundland girl. Grace Darling, with a fascinating museum and impressive monument at Bamburgh, suffers no such neglect.

During World War Two another Newfoundland lighthouse keeper's daughter played a role in the rescue of a group of seamen. In October 1941 the German submarine U-208, under the command of Alfred Schlieper, was sent to the North Atlantic to sink allied merchant ships. November 2, at 5:26 a.m., Schlieper sighted the SS *Larpool* about 250 miles east-southeast of Cape Race. The merchant vessel had strayed from a convoy bound from Halifax to Britain. A torpedo from the U-boat scored a direct hit.

Late on the night of November 13, eleven days after the sinking, little Irene Dicks, the daughter of John Dicks, the lightkeeper at Tide's Point in Placentia Bay, eight miles from the town of Burin, saw a flare in the sky. Instead of ignoring it as a child might, she ran to tell her father what she had seen. Mr. Dicks and his assistant, William J. Power of Mortier, searched the bay until they located a lifeboat with five exhausted men on board. They were the captain, mate and three seamen of the sunken SS *Larpool* who were immediately transported from the lighthouse to the cottage hospital in Burin. December 11, 1941, the U-208 was depth charged and sunk by HMS *Bluebell* west of Gibraltar. The *Larpool* was the only ship the submarine ever sank. Little Irene Dicks is today Mrs. Charles Pearcey.

Chapter Seven

An Outline of Labrador History

Although he never set foot on shore the first European credited with the discovery of Labrador is Biarni Herjulfson in A.D. 986. When Leif Ericsson landed there afterwards he named it Markland. With the departure of the Vikings from the shores of North America, the place was forgotten for nearly 500 years.

Some historians claim a Labrador landfall for John Cabot in 1497, but because of the way in which his son, Sebastian, deliberately garbled accounts of his father's voyages, it is as difficult to prove as the claims of Newfoundland and Cape Breton to being Cabot's first landfall.

In the year 1500, two Portuguese explorers arrived upon the scene. In October 1499, King Manuel gave a humble lavrador (husbandman), named Joao Fernandes, who farmed out his property while he was away exploring, permission to search for and discover islands in the west Atlantic. His voyage in 1500 is not documented, except on maps, where we learn he reached at least as far as Cape Farewell, Greenland, that summer and that he called the great island Tiera del Lavrador, Land of the Husbandman (farmer). In time all the territory in the Atlantic north of Newfoundland became known on maps as Lavrador.

That same summer, another Portuguese explorer, Gaspar Corte Real, also sailed west with the permission of King Manuel. He discovered land at about latitude 50°N, "a land that was very cool and with big trees", which he named Terra Verde. There can be no doubt that what he found was Newfoundland. If it was not already sighted by Cabot, then Corte Real must be credited with its discovery. After returning to Lisbon in the autumn, Gaspar set out to return to his new land in mid-May 1501 with three ships. Two got back to Portugal later in the year, but the explorer was never seen again. According to some accounts Corte Real sailed north and was lost in a gale off the Labrador coast.

Whether Labrador was rediscovered after Viking times by

Cabot, Fernandes, Corte Real or even Jacques Cartier, we will probably never know with certainty, but we do know that the place got its name from Joao Fernandes when later geographers shifted the name, by which the lands of the North Atlantic had become known, to the continental area of eastern North America which is still known as Labrador.

From the early years of the 16th century Labrador was visited by an endless stream of explorers, adventurers and fishermen. In 1527 John Rut reached the place on his way from England "to seke strange regions" at the behest of Henry VIII. Master Rut, whose instructions were to find the Northwest Passage, had little taste for Arctic adventuring and after sailing north as far as Hawke Bay without finding the passage, headed south for the West Indies via Newfoundland. There is no record of his having gone ashore anywhere. August 3, he wrote King Henry from St. John's "that we have found many great Ilands of Ice and deepe water, we found no sounding."

During the first week of June 1534, Jacques Cartier put an end to speculation about landing on the coast of Labrador by going ashore at some spot on the Strait of Belle Isle. He was not complimentary about the territory he surveyed south from Red Bay. In his "Premier Relation" he wrote of the country, "Were the soil as good as the harbours, it would be fine; but this should not be called Terra Neuve, being composed of stones and frightful rocks and uneven places; for on this entire northern coast I saw not one cartload of earth, though I landed in many places. Except for Blanc Sablon there is nothing but moss and stunted shrubs. To conclude, I am inclined to regard this land as the one God gave to Cain." Unfortunately for Labrador's image, Cartier's epitaph, "the land God gave to Cain", was to endure until the present century. There is no doubt that the glacier-scraped granite shore and shallow valleys of stunted spruce trees gave a desolate impression, especially in the spring ice and fogs. Audubon called it a "poor, rugged, miserable country." Unseen by these men were the endless miles of beautiful white sands further north, the limitless stands of green timber sweeping over game-filled mountains, the wide river valleys and the awesome great falls.

There were Basque whalers who undoubtedly went ashore on the coast a decade or two before Cartier. By the middle of the 16th century, they were pursuing herds of giant mammals in the Straits of Belle Isle, processing the carcasses on the spot and shipping the refined products back to Europe. The discovery in Spanish archives in the late 1970s of a last will and testament drafted at Red Bay, June 22, 1577, by Juan Martinez de Lorrume, as well as other documents, led to the finding of a wealth of artifacts on Saddle Island in Red Bay by a Memorial University archaeological team in 1978. About 100 meters offshore the wreck of a Spanish galleon, the *San Juan*, was discovered. It went to the bottom in a squall over 400 years ago. The ship is in a very good state of preservation. The oak planks used to build the 70-man vessel are in excellent condition.

The documents found in Spain show that as many as 800 men and boys may have lived at Red Bay in the height of the season. There were no women, as the settlement was only occupied in summer. One document shows that two of the whalers were killed by Indians and another records one of the first business transactions ever noted in Canada when Joannes deLecho of Chateau Bay purchased four rowboats in 1572. The departure of the humpback whales and the 1588 recall of all Spanish ships to form the great Armada put an end to Basque ventures in Labrador. Red Bay was afterwards so named because of the thousands of broken red tiles left behind by the whalers and found by British fishermen.

Martin Frobisher revived English interest when he visited the territory in 1576, 1577 and 1578 in an attempt to exploit mining, while seeking the elusive Northwest Passage. He was followed in less than ten years by John Davis. In the same decade in which Sir Humphrey Gilbert sailed into St. John's harbour and claimed Newfoundland in the name of Queen Elizabeth I, Davis touched at Sandwich Bay and sailed north along the coast, noting that the country had a great store of birds "as fezant, partridge, Barbary hennes or the like, wild geese, ducks...pleasant and very full of fayre woods...great abundance of cod...and divers fisher men that were with me say that they never saw a...better skull of fish in their lives...." In 1587, in the

42

first recorded reference to English fishing off the Labrador coast, John Davis says he left two ships with orders not to depart until his return, but that within "sixteene dayes the two shippes had finished their voyage, and so presently departed for England". On his quest to seek out the Northwest Passage, Davis discovered and named Cape Chidley at the northern tip of Labrador after a neighbour of his back in Devon, John Chidley. He is himself remembered in the name Davis Strait between Baffin Island and Greenland. After clarifying much arctic geography north of Labrador, in 1592 Davis discovered the Falkland Islands. He lost his life in the East Indies fighting Japanese pirates in 1605.

Bradore, which the French called Brest, was much frequented by them as a fishing resort from the early 1500s. Lewis Roberts in the *Dictionary of Commerce*, printed in London in 1638, said of the place, "It was the chief town of New France, the residence of the Governor, Almoner, and other public officers; the French draw from thence large quantities of baccalao, whale fins, train [oil], together with castor [beaver] and other valuable furs."

By the mid-1600s the place was in decay, but in 1704 it gained a new lease on life with the grant of four leagues of the coast, including the community of Brest, to Augustin Legardeur, the Siegneur de Courtemanche, who is said to have developed it into a town of 200 houses with as many as 1000 winter residents. Courtemanche was interested in furs, fish and seal products and he ruled the territory for thirteen years, until his death in 1717. He was succeeded by his son-in-law, de Brouage, who resided there for forty-one years, by which time the Seven Years' War was underway. When de Brouage abandoned claims to Brest (Bradore) the community and surrounding coast was monopolized by a company in Quebec called the "Quebec Company".

April 20, 1705, a land grant of almost the whole of the Great Northern peninsula of Newfoundland was made to Sieur Francois Hazeur. This was followed May 18, 1713, by another grant to one Pierre Constantin of all of what is today western Labrador. These grants are today recorded in the archives of

Laval University in Quebec City.

The abundance of cod in Labrador waters, discovered by Davis and other English navigators, was not exploited by British merchants until the end of the 18th century, when the Grand Banks and other southern fishing grounds became crowded with European fishermen. The first authentic account of English interest in the region occurs after the Treaty of Paris in 1763, which ended the Seven Years' War and French dreams of an empire in North America. The territory was annexed to the Government of Newfoundland, including "all the coast of Labrador, from the entrance of Hudson's Straits to the River St. John's, opposite the west end of the Island of Anticosti, including that island, with any other small islands on the said coast of Labrador, also the island of Madeleine, in the Gulf of St. Lawrence, and all the forts and garrisons erected or established, or shall be erected or established, in the said Island, or on the coast of Labrador, within the limits aforesaid." The terms of the treaty gave Newfoundland undisputed legal claim not only to what is today Labrador, but a large part of the present province of Quebec, plus the islands south of the St. Lawrence.

The Governor of Newfoundland, Sir Hugh Palliser, did not hesitate long before asserting his authority over the territory. In 1764 he ordered work to start on the construction of Fort York at Chateau Bay. It was completed September 7, 1767. Unfortunately, his treatment of those planters holding grants in Labrador from the Government of Canada led to complaints in London. In an about-face in 1774 the British Government, without consulting Newfoundland, placed the whole of the territory under the jurisdiction of what had been old provincial Quebec. However, effective control by Quebec did not reach beyond the Straits of Belle Isle. Northward the annexation was ignored and the Governor of Newfoundland continued to watch over the area until 1809, when the British Government properly returned Labrador to the authority of Newfoundland. England's high-handed action in abrogating the terms of the Treaty of Paris was to cause Newfoundland serious problems over Quebec territorial claims in Labrador by the beginning of the 20th century.

Although, by his own admission, Captain George Cartwright was by no means the first Englishman to settle on the coast of Upper Labrador, he was its most important pioneer and his detailed journal of life there is an invaluable document. After having served the British Army as a captain in the 37th Foot, the 30-year old soldier arrived on the Labrador coast in 1770 and settled at Cape Charles. He had been attracted to the area when he went there, with a shooting party bent on pleasure, in the ship of his brother, who was a naval officer on a vessel that had been ordered to the Newfoundland station. He became friendly with the Eskimos who settled in his community at Cape Charles and demanded he feed them all winter. From his diary we learn that he acted as doctor, clergyman and judge. In the latter capacity he was given to the lash and often carried out his own sentences. He did a brisk trade with the natives and at one time took a party of two Eskimos, their wives and a little girl, to London. Their astonished faces created an enormous novelty in England and all went well until they prepared to return home. Smallpox broke out among them, killing four. The fifth carried the germ of the disease to Labrador and died later.

In 1775, Cartwright decided to move further north and settled at a place called Cartwright in Sandwich Bay. During the American War of Independence, he calculated he lost $70,000 worth of goods to deserters and American privateers. When one of his ships, carrying his whole stock of fish, oil and furs, was captured, he was completely ruined. One of his creditors accused him of fraud and seized his property in England. He returned home in 1786, took the case to the law courts, and eventually won it, but his setbacks made it impossible for him to return to Labrador. He became a barrack master in Nottingham, where he died in 1819.

While George Cartwright was opening up the Upper Labrador, the Governor of Newfoundland continued to fortify the coast. Palliser sent his protege, Captain James Cook, (who was afterwards to win immortality by his exploits in New Zealand and Hawaii), to survey the coast from 1763 to 1767. Spear Harbour was fortified in 1780 with guns and ammunition sent from St. John's for the purpose. By September of 1794,

Temple Bay was described as being defended by four forts. The following year, the French made an attack on the coast, wrought cruel havoc among the fishermen, capturing a number of fishing and trading ships. Fort York was bombarded into silence. The British set fire to all the buildings and took to the woods until the French departed with their prizes.

The rule of law reached Labrador June 17, 1824, when a Court of Civil Jurisdiction for the Coast was established by an Act of the British Government. That same year, Governor Cochrane issued a proclamation giving it effect and stipulating that sessions of the Court be held at Invuctoke, Huntingdon Harbour, Venison Island, Cape St. Francis Harbour, Cape St. Charles Harbour, Chateau Bay and L'Anse-Au-Loup. Captain William Patterson was appointed judge and George Simms, clerk. Bryan Robinson, afterwards a judge of the Supreme Court in St. John's (who gave his name to Robinson's Hill), was appointed Sheriff of Labrador in 1829 and was succeeded in the office by Elias Rendell in 1833. The Court was abolished by an Act of the Newfoundland Legislature in 1834.

Duties were collected on the coast by Elias Rendell in the summer of 1841, but the procedure was discontinued until 1856 when a second attempt at enforcing Customs regulations was made with as little success. In 1863, "An Act to provide for the Collection of Revenue and for the better Administration of Justice at the Labrador" was passed by the Newfoundland Legislature and James Winter (whose son, Sir James, became Prime Minister of Newfoundland) was appointed Collector for the Coast. Benjamin Sweetland was made Judge for the Labrador Coast. This Court was discontinued in 1874, but later revived, with F.J. Morris as judge.

As early as May 2, 1670, King Charles II granted to the Hudson's Bay Company a comprehensive charter giving that concern, amongst other things, possession of all that portion of Labrador drained by rivers falling into Hudson's Bay and Hudson's Straits. In 1839, a veteran trader who worked as a factor for the Hudson's Bay Company became the first white man to discover the Great Falls on the Hamilton River, now Churchill Falls on the Churchill River. The dour Scot was named John McLean. In 1973, a lawyer in Sarnia, Ontario, Andrew Lang, purchased some antiques, including a camera and glass negatives. One of the wrappers contained this information; "Enclosed negative of John McClean who was for twenty-five years with the Hudson's Bay Company and was the first white man to discover the Grand Falls on the Hamilton River in Labrador in 1839...." The picture was taken in the 1860s by Thomas Cannon and is now in the possession of CFLCo.

An Act was passed by the Newfoundland Legislature in 1881 regulating the carrying of passengers on steamers and sailing vessels between Newfoundland and Labrador. It provided separate quarters for females, limited the number of passengers to one person for each registered ton and stipulated for adequate lifeboat accommodation. Given the stormy nature of the coast and the vast armada of overcrowded and overloaded vessels from the island of Newfoundland that sailed up and down Labrador, it seems miraculous that there was not a greater loss of life than there was over the years.

By the middle of the 19th century, as many as 30,000 transients out of a Newfoundland population of less than 150,000 prosecuted the Northern cod fishery each year. In 1885, a terrific storm that swept over the Labrador coast from October 11th to the 13th caused sad havoc to life and property and brought mourning and misery to thousands of people. About eighty fishing craft were lost and some seventy men, women and children perished. A church was blown down in the gale, which was especially severe in the neighbourhood of Indian Harbour. Many famous St. John's firms, such as Job Bros. & Co., Baine, Johnson & Co., J. & W. Stewart, P. Rogerson & Son, reported the loss of ships. P. & L. Tessier lost three of their vessels. The *Hope* and the *Release* foundered at White Bears with fourteen drowned in the former and twenty-five drowned in the latter, mostly women and children.

In 1902, a north northeast gale of terrible violence struck the coast on September 24th and lasted three days. It was especially severe on the 24th and 25th, devastating communities from Horse Harbour to Nain. Only the fact that the tide was low saved hundreds of thousands of dollars worth of property, and possibly many lives. Seven fishermen drowned in the loss of one schooner in the Straits. Eighteen Newfoundland vessels were reported wrecked. The SS *Virginia Lake*, which was sheltered from the storm at Windy Tickle, landed 137 people at Tilt Cove from nine lost schooners.

Saturday night, July 25, 1908, a storm came on along the Labrador coast that raged heavily all day Sunday. Worst hit was Tinkers Harbour near Holton, where seven vessels were driven ashore or foundered. In all, forty ships were said to have been lost between Indian Harbour and King's Bay. The SS *Virginia Lake* was again on the scene. This time she was anchored at Battle Harbour. There was a report in St. John's that she was on her way home with 980 shipwrecked men from Bonavista Bay who wired Prime Minister Morris demanding they be put ashore at Wesleyville. The *Daily News* corrected the number to 165 and the *Evening Telegram* placed it at 150. After that storm, the cruiser HMS *Fiona* brought 111 shipwrecked men back to Newfoundland. Six fishermen were drowned from two schooners at St. Paul's Island.

The last important event in pre-20th century Labrador history occurred in the summer of 1892, when a young doctor from England, Wilfred Grenfell, paid his first visit to the coast in the hospital ship, *Albert,* and spent three months among the people whose lives he was to change for all time.

Chapter Eight

Peter Easton — Pirate Admiral of the West Atlantic

Peter Easton may be ranked with Captain Morgan and Captain Kidd as one of the three great pirates of the west Atlantic. The son of an old and respected English family, he had an ancestor, Bishop Easton, who rose to the rank of cardinal in the 14th century and was involved in a plot to overthrow Pope Urban VI. Arrested, imprisoned and tortured, we are told, Cardinal Easton was reinstated by Urban's successor, Boniface IX.

The pirate Admiral's name is first recorded in 1602 when, in the service of Queen Elizabeth, he commanded a Royal Navy convoy for the Newfoundland fishing fleet. The following year, James I succeeded to the throne and one of his first actions was to abolish British sea power. The navy was disbanded and letters granting a licence to privateers to fit out ships for the capture of enemy merchant vessels were withdrawn. Naval officers had neither ships nor pay, but the King allowed them to retain their ranks. Without incomes, many of these men turned to piracy to earn a living and Peter Easton is said to have been one of them.

Between 1603, when he disappears to become a privateer, and 1610 when we next hear of him, Easton built up one of the largest pirate fleets in the world. He commanded 40 ships operating off the coast of Cornwall and held up all traffic in the Bristol Channel at the mouth of the Avon River, so that the merchants of Bristol had to appeal for help to the Lord Admiral, the Earl of Nottingham.

The pirate fleet was under the general protection of the Kelligrews, a powerful family which virtually ruled western Cornwall from Pendennis Castle in Falmouth. John Kelligrew was tried and acquitted for treason when it was found he had attempted to sell England to Spain for £10,000 in gold at the time of the second Spanish Armada. Although he was not convicted, through influence in high places, there is no doubt of his guilt.

49

Under the care and protection of the Kelligrews, western Cornwall became a haven for pirates, later immortalized by Gilbert and Sullivan in the comic opera *The Pirates of Penzance*. The family supplied any vessel which flew the "Jolly Roger", in those days a plain black flag. The skull and cross-bones were a later addition.

The Earl of Nottingham was powerless to do anything against Easton, since he was an admiral without a Navy. Instead, he ordered a young man named Harry Mainwaring, later to achieve fame as a privateer, to go in pursuit of the Pirate Admiral and bring him captive to London to answer charges against him. Hearing of this, Peter Easton decided not to commit High Treason by warring with the Royal Navy in English waters and disbanded his fleet. Taking ten of his best ships with highly experienced crews, he set sail for Newfoundland and arrived in Conception Bay in the spring of 1610. The island was to be his headquarters for several years, as he plundered the merchant shipping of England's enemies on the High Seas from the West Indies to the Azores, and as far east as the coast of Guinea in Africa. It was claimed by Captain John Smith, of "Pocahontas" fame, that over the years Easton recruited between 15,000 and 20,000 fishermen in Newfoundland to man his ships. If this is so, he must have added another 15 to 20 captured vessels to his fleet.

The settlement of Harbour Grace is said to have been given its name by the French pirate, Jean Ango of Dieppe, who helped King Francis I build Havre de Grace (now Le Havre) at the mouth of the River Seine as a deepwater harbour for Paris. It was while plundering from Newfoundland to the Antilles and back again that Ango transferred the name of Havre de Grace to the Newfoundland town we now call Harbour Grace, a place Peter Easton made his West Atlantic headquarters.

While John Guy's colonists were busy at Cupids in 1610, trying to establish the first colony in what is today English Canada, not many miles away, at Harbour Grace, Peter Easton and his men were building a pirate fort at the harbour entrance with a lookout tower and a series of shore batteries below, armed with powerful cannon taken from captured ships. This was the first fort in Newfoundland, erected half a century before the British Government decided to man and fortify the island.

October 12, 1612, John Guy, having established his colony at Cupids, visited the nearby port of Harbour Grace, where he found the place protected by the pirate fort. Easton was away at the time and the two men did not meet until later, when the pirate captured and released one of Guy's ships off St. John's.

The recruitment of pirate crews in Newfoundland at the time was not difficult. Gosse tells us, in his *History of Piracy*:

> To the island there came each season hundreds of fishing boats, bringing numbers of poor men from the west of England who received low wages from the contractors and had to pay their own passages home at the end of the season.
>
> Their work, fishing, or else the slitting and drying of the cod on shore, was very hard, and their only relaxation the drinking of blackstrap, a villainous concoction of rum, molasses and chowder beer.
>
> The blackstrap cost money, as did the bare necessities of life, so that when the time came to return to England, many men had not enough money left to pay their passages. It was such unfortunates as these that the pirates looked to manning their ships on the principle that beggars cannot be choosers.

It is easy to see how Newfoundland, especially the harbours of Conception Bay and the Southern Shore, became a favorite hunting ground for men and ships as piracy grew into a great trade.

In his diary, John Guy records October 12, 1612:

> That night by sayling, and rowing we came to Harbour de Gras as farre in as ye Pirates Forte, where ye banke shippe roade, where we remayned until ye 17th day of ye sayde month, and in ye meane time did bring ye banke shippe ashoare, land ye salt upon ye highest part of ye ground there aboutes putting yt up in a round heape, and burning yt to preserve yt, two anchors, and two old junkes we left upon ye beache, ye quantity of salt was about fifteen tonnes."

It would appear from this diary entry that Guy was

welcomed by whoever was manning the fort at Harbour Grace and permitted to set up a salt store on shore for the curing of cod. Presumably the salt was sent to Harbour Grace for safe keeping during the winter, as it was the only fortified harbour in Newfoundland, even if the fortifications were those of English pirates.

This apparent harmony between the settlers and pirate crews did not last. Sir Richard Whitbourne tells us that in the year 1612, Peter Easton arrived at Harbour Grace and stole five ships, 100 pieces of ordnance and goods to the value of $10,400. He also took or induced 500 English fishermen to join him in piracy. On shore his men did great harm, robbing goods, burning down the forests, and committing murders and theft. Whitbourne was made a prisoner and kept 11 weeks, during which time the Pirate Admiral asked Sir Richard to obtain a pardon for him in England. That year Easton plundered 30 English vessels in the harbour of St. John's, as well as a number of French and Portuguese ships in harbours along the Southern Shore to Ferryland and Aquaforte.

It must be said for Peter Easton that he still did nothing to harm settlement or the colonists. His raids were on the property of west country merchants and their ships. On one occasion, some settlers gave Easton a gift of two pigs. In spite of Whitbourne's claim that the pirates committed murders and theft, there was only one clash with the colonists and in it one of them was wounded by error. Whitbourne states that in spite of his success as a privateer, and the great wealth he had amassed, Easton was consumed "with a longing desire and full expectation to be called home." When Sir Richard was released from captivity in Newfoundland and finally arrived in England, he discovered that a pardon had already been granted by the king in February 1612, but it had never reached Easton because Captain Roger Middleton, the commissioner who was to deliver the pardon, did not arrive at Harbour Grace until after the Pirate Admiral left for the Caribbean in search of Spanish treasure ships. According to Whitbourne, Easton "lost that hope by too much delaying of time by him who carried the pardon." It was re-granted on November 26th.

While Easton was away, his fort at Harbour Grace was captured by French Basques who sailed out to meet him on his return. He had with him a Spanish treasure galleon, the *San Sebastian*, captured in the Caribbean. An engagement was fought near the harbour mouth and in the battle all the Basque ships were sunk or captured. The warship, *St. Malo,* which led the French squadron, was driven ashore on a small rocky islet known as Easton's Isle, now corrupted to Easter Rock. The English pirates lost 47 men in the engagement. They buried their dead at Bear Cove in a place which became known as the Pirates Graveyard. The *San Sebastian* was beached and stripped. Her anchor was recovered in 1855 by Captain William Stevenson.

After the Basque engagement, the pirate admiral moved his headquarters from Harbour Grace to Ferryland where, it is claimed, he remained from 1612 to 1614. When he did not receive the pardon he expected by March, 1613, Easton decided to abandon Newfoundland for Africa, but first he sailed out of Ferryland to conduct a vendetta against Spain. Some of his ships and men may have remained at Ferryland until the following year. In command of a powerful fleet, said to consist of as many as 40 ships, he sailed south and attacked the Spanish colony founded by Ponce de Leon on the Caribbean island of Porto Rico. First he captured a fort commanded by the governor and then took the stronger military bastion of Morro Castle. Thirteen years earlier, another English pirate, who was to win more reverent fame as Sir Francis Drake, was defeated in his attempts to take the castle and capture the island. The fall of the invincible fort gave the pirate from Newfoundland his greatest moment of glory, but it was quickly forsaken for the gold of the Porto Rican mines.

While all this was happening, Easton was still obsessed with the desire to obtain a pardon and be accepted by the English court. He sent one of his lieutenants, Captain John Harvey, home to England with "considerable sums of money" and a petition. Harvey landed in Ireland and forwarded the money and petition to the Kelligrews who passed everything into the king's hands. The pardon was quickly granted by the avaricious James, but Easton appears not to have been told for some considerable time, if at all.

In the late summer of 1614, as he was preparing to abandon Newfoundland and the Caribbean for Africa, one of his scout ships brought word that the Spanish Plate Fleet was on its way from South America to Spain via the Azores. Easton paid off most of his crews, keeping only 10 ships. With these he set out to try and intercept the Spanish fleet. He deployed his squadron in a wide arc to the west and south of the Azores until his prey was sighted. Details of the battle have not been recorded, but we know that Easton soundly defeated the enemy and reached Tunis in north Africa with four Spanish treasure ships as prizes.

The Bey of Tunis, a man who was one of the most powerful rulers in the Moslem world, welcomed the Pirate Admiral and tried to talk him into taking charge of his Tunisian fleet. It is even said the Bey offered to divide his kingdom with Easton if he would convert to the Moslem faith and become Admiral of the fleet, but the story appears to be more legend than fact. Easton's contemporary, the pirate Sir Harry Mainwaring, discredits the story, while claiming the Bey of Tunis made him the same offer, with the understanding he might remain a Christian and could return to England whenever he chose.

Within the year Easton paid off the rest of his men, disposed of his ships and retired across the Mediterranean to Ville Franche, where he settled under the protection of the Duke of Savoy, in what is now the Principality of Monaco. Sir William Mason, the Admiral of the Narrow Seas under James I, and Captain John Smith, both claim that because of his great wealth, Easton was able to purchase from the nearly bankrupt Duke, the title of Marquis of Savoy. His wealth has been estimated as high as two million pounds, having an approximate value today of $100 million.

While in the employ of the Duke of Savoy, Peter Easton distinguished himself by his placement and management of the guns during the siege of the Duchy of Mantua. He returned to Ville Franche in 1620, married a wealthy woman and acquired a magnificent palace in what is today Monte Carlo. After that the great Pirate Admiral, then about 40 years old, vanishes from the stage of world history. All we know of his last years is Sir

Richard Whitbourne's claim that he "lived rich."

Rev. E. Hunt, the Newfoundland historian, says of Peter Easton in the *Dictionary of Canadian Biography*:

"Easton was the leading corsair of his day and one of the most famous in the whole annals of piracy. He possessed all the requisite skills for his infamous trade, but was neither a blood-thirsty monster nor a swashbuckling cut-throat. On the contrary, he proved himself an outstanding navigator, an able, brave and bold seaman, an expert tactician, and highly competitive in gun-laying. He controlled such seapower that no sovereign or state could afford to ignore him and he was never overtaken or captured by any fleet commissioned to hunt him down."

Chapter Nine

The Garrison Mutiny and the Girl from Fogo

Maurice Fitzgerald, an Anglo-Irish invader of Ireland, died in 1176, having founded a noble family which descended in two branches from his sons, the earls of Kildare and Desmond. Lord Edward Fitzgerald was born to the twentieth Earl of Kildare in 1763. At the age of sixteen he was fighting with the British Army in the American Revolution. He was later expelled from the forces for republicanism.

The United Irishmen was the name given to a political organization founded in 1791 by Wolfe Tone. It spread rapidly and was suppressed in 1794. After that it operated as a secret revolutionary body and sought aid in France. Following his adventures in America, Lord Edward joined the United Irishmen and the 35-year-old patriot was a leader in the French-aided Irish rebellion of 1798. Four days before the appointed date of the uprising, Fitzgerald was betrayed and captured. A few days later he died of wounds in Newgate Prison. The English put down the rising and captured the leaders. Wolfe Tone committed suicide by stabbing himself in the neck with a penknife when he found out he was to be hanged like a traitor, instead of shot like a soldier. The '98 Rising was later to have repercussions in Newfoundland. The trouble began in 1797. It started with the discovery that the garrison food supply of pork had gone bad.

October 2, 1797, the first military food supplies for the season were drawn from the Commissary Stores at St. John's and the pork issued was so putrid, a report on its condition was sent to Colonel Skinner. He reported to his superiors that a man named Ainsworth "peeled the skin of two pieces and thrust his fingers into the meat which, I believe, could not have been the case with sound meat, nearly all pieces were quite yellow." This, coupled with other abuses, led 22 men to desert the Royal Newfoundland Regiment that year. The rate of desertion was becoming alarming.

A Court of Enquiry was held into the putrid meat supply and it found that out of 1,440 lbs. of pork, only 276 lbs. were fit to eat. As well, 2,740 lbs. of flour had to be thrown into the harbour. These rations were not replaced and in conditions of near starvation the soldiers struggled through the winter. By January 15, 1798, all available food in St. John's had been bought or requisitioned, and there was only a 10 weeks' supply left in the military stores. To add to this trouble, on March 24, at 2:30 in the morning, a fire broke out in Fort William. In less than half an hour the eastern front of the Garrison was in flames, which consumed the whole of the officers' barracks and 6 of the barrack rooms used by the soldiers. No lives were lost but all the medical supplies of the surgeon, Dr. Ogden, and much bedding, utensils, and stores were totally destroyed. The whole of Fort William would have gone except for the efforts of the officers and crew of HMS *Shark* and the inhabitants of the town.

Only a small quantity of lumber was available for immediate repairs. (The weather was infinitely too cold, the snow and ice too deep, to allow the dispossessed soldiers to encamp.) There was serious overcrowding of quarters and many soldiers gave voice to their misery and discontent.

Governor Waldegrave, who was wintering in London, appears to have received the news with apathy. His mind seems to have been more occupied with the rebellion of the United Irishmen under Wolfe Tone that had broken out in Ireland. Fearing sympathy with the uprising might enkindle a similar event in Newfoundland, Waldegrave urged the Duke of Portland to order the Chief Justice of Newfoundland, D'Ewes Coke, to take up permanent residence in St. John's, because "nine tenths of the inhabitants of this Island are either natives of Ireland or immediate descendants from them, and that the whole of these are of the Roman Catholic persuasion". The governor added, "it is therefore to the wise and vigilant administration of the civil power that we must look to preserve peace and good order (the present times considered) in this settlement". To this end, he cultivated the friendship of the Roman Catholic Bishop at St. John's, Dr. O'Donel, who had no sympathy with rebellions or the rebellious.

While attempting to do what he could to further guarantee tranquility, His Excellency issued a number of unpopular orders to limit the pleasures of the troops. He forbade unauthorized visits to grog shops and bawdy houses and virtually forbade a favourite pastime of the soldiers, the keeping of pets. He ordered "all dogs straggling about the Fort after Gun Fire to be bayonetted by the Centinals, or hanged by the Guard". These repressive measures, along with continuing conditions of near starvation, increased desertions among a garrison of mostly Newfoundland Irishmen and kept away volunteers. It created the atmosphere of discontent and rebelliousness the governor was hoping to avoid.

During the winter of 1798-99, Brigadier General William Skerret was appointed Commanding Officer of troops in Newfoundland, under supervision of the Commander-in-Chief in Nova Scotia. He arrived in St. John's in May, direct from Ireland, where as Colonel of "Skerrets Horse" he had played an important role in helping to successfully put down the United Irishmen's Rebellion of Tone and Lord Edward Fitzgerald.

The main problem in 1799 would seem to have been desertions from the navy. The governor complained that men had been enticed away for purposes of manning vessels that were to sail to Europe. In October, he issued a notice promising that if any seaman or other person or persons belonging to His Majesty's squadron, or His Majesty's Royal Newfoundland Regiment be found on any vessel or vessels in the ports of Newfoundland, the Master of the vessel should answer at his peril and be punished to the utmost severity of the law.

Unknown to Waldegrave, fanatical members of the United Irish, in strong sympathy with their homeland's bid for independence from England, following William Pitt's blind refusal to grant Catholic emancipation, were administering the secret oath of the United Irishmen and urging the regiment to mutiny and murder their English officers. The plot was hatched during the winter of 1799-1800.

The first symptoms that something was afoot appeared in the latter part of February, 1800, when some anonymous papers were posted about St. John's at night, threatening the persons and property of the magistrates if they persisted in enforcing a proclamation they had published respecting hogs going at large, contrary to a presentiment of the grand jury. One hundred guineas reward was offered for the capture of the persons responsible for the posters. The inhabitants offered 200 guineas more, but without effect.

On April 20th the first signs of real discontent among the garrison appeared. It being Sunday, the troops were paraded to worship, the English to church and the Irish to chapel. It was a fine day, but it was noted that some of the regiment went through their exercises in a strangely careless manner. Dr. O'Donel, who had become Roman Catholic bishop in 1796, learned that there was reason to suspect that one of the two companies on Signal Hill was planning open rebellion. The information is said to have been given to the prelate by the wife of one of the men involved who became frightened of the outcome, and went to the Bishop seeking his advice. This was evidently done outside confession which would have sealed the man's lips. The French Revolution had filled O'Donel with revulsion for all opposition to lawful authority. He went immediately to General Skerret with the information given him by the woman and the General kept the regiment at exercises all day Sunday. This prevented anything happening that day and the emergency seemed to abate.

On the 23rd, Captain Tremblett reported five or six of the soldiers to their commanding officer for being idle and dirty, and confined another for being drunk. He told the culprits he would see justice done them. They concluded Tremblett knew of their postponed scheme for an uprising in the colony and decided it must be on the following day. This information was also passed to the Bishop, who again conveyed it to the General.

Between 40 and 50 men of the Royal Newfoundland Regiment were to desert with their arms on the night of April 25th. They were to rendezvous about 11:00 at a powder shed behind Fort Townshend, on the east corner of present day Belvedere Street and Hayward Avenue. A party for Colonel

Skinner was quickly planned and held at Fort William. It continued until a late hour, preventing the men who planned to desert from leaving for their rendezvous unnoticed. For some reason, probably the vigilance of their officers, the troops at Fort Townshend also failed to get away to join the mutineers.

Nobody was able to get word to the troops on Signal Hill that the uprising at Fort William and Fort Townshend had been frustrated. A group of soldiers left there for the rendezvous, but within three minutes their absence was noticed by Captain Tremblett, who gave the alarm. In all, only 19 of the men had got off. The others had no time. Ten of the deserters were soon captured, while the remainder fled into the woods. Two more were apparently apprehended the following day. Justice was swift. Five of the twelve were sentenced to be hanged and the remainder to be shot. A gallows was erected at the spot where they were to meet at the powder shed and the hangings carried out. The remaining seven, and another four who were captured after the hasty trials, were sent to Halifax to set an example there, in case there were any in sympathy.

July 7, 1800, the inhabitants of that Nova Scotia town awoke to the sound of a marching military band playing funeral marches. Behind it came a cart draped in black, carrying eleven black coffins followed by the eleven mutineers from Newfoundland. The whole of the garrison, along with hundreds of inhabitants, waited atop Citadel Hill to watch the early morning executions. However, in a show of liberality, His Royal Highness, the Duke of Kent, then in command in Nova Scotia, commuted eight of the death sentences to life imprisonment. By 6:40 a.m. the remaining three were hanged and pronounced dead.

The mutiny had also sounded the death knell of the Royal Newfoundland Regiment. Except for two companies of picked men, the whole was shipped to Halifax, where it remained under the watchful eye of the Royal Commander-in-Chief until it was disbanded in 1802. Newfoundlanders were not to be trusted in their own country.

It is generally agreed that sympathy with the lost cause of the United Irishmen was merely the catalyst in the attempted

Newfoundland mutiny of the regiment in 1800. The poor living conditions of the troops and frequent periods of near starvation contributed to their unrest, as did the near slavery of the fishermen and labourers who were kept in debt to their employers year after year. There were other factors, such as the denial of religious and political freedoms, the refusal to allow Catholic as well as Dissenter clergy to marry their flock or bury their dead, laws which forbade the granting of property rights or the free movement of the inhabitants, and a host of bothersome pieces of legislation which made any betterment of the lot of the poor impossible. Some of the mutineers had a vague idea of linking the colony to the recently independent republic to the south, but that would have proven an impossible dream, for had the rebellion succeeded, it would undoubtedly have been put down immediately by the Duke of Kent, with troops from Halifax. In most countries, people who lead attempted coups against repressive authority are remembered as heroes. The men of 1800 are almost completely forgotten.

The real link between Newfoundland and the Rising of '98 was not so much the St. John's mutiny, as Lord Edward Fitzgerald through his wife, Pamela, one of the great European beauties of her day. She was painted by Romney and a dazzling portrait of her hangs in the collection of the National Gallery, Dublin. Leinster House, the great mansion over which she presided as hostess, is now the Parliament House of the Irish Republic.

According to the Fitzgerald family, Lord Edward's wife was the daughter of the French Duke and Duchess of Orleans. It has been whispered into the legend that she was, in fact, the illegitimate child of the French king placed in the family of the Duke to disguise a royal indiscretion. The facts of history seem to indicate that Lady Pamela Fitzgerald, instead of being the offspring of the nobility, was actually Ann Syms, born to an unmarried woman in a winter tilt on Fogo Island, in 1773.

At the time of Ann's birth, there was a small fort on Fogo Island with six cannon. A naval officer named Jeremiah Coughlan was stationed there to organize a force of fishermen to repel any French or American invasion attempt. Coughlan took Nancy Syms (also spelled Sims), the daughter of one of the resident fishermen, into his service in the spring of 1771. He was known to be the father of Ann, who was born out of wedlock two years later. She is called Little Nancy in some accounts. Coughlan acknowledged the paternity of the child and took both mother and daughter with him to England, where they were soon abandoned. The mother went into domestic service at Christ Church in Devonshire.

When Ann was about six years old, the Duke of Orleans wrote from France to a friend in England, asking if he could find a young English girl as a permanent companion for his children. The friend, who was in Christ Church at the time, knew Ann's circumstances and persuaded Nancy Syms to part with her child. The girl was sent to France in charge of a valet, along with a blood mare. An accompanying letter said, "I am sending your Highness the finest mare and prettiest little girl in all England."

Taken into the care of Madame de Genlis, and renamed Pamela, she soon became one of the Duke's family. The mother was paid twenty-five pounds to resign all claim to the child. The girl from Fogo was educated at Belle Chase with princes and princesses of the blood as companions. When the French Revolution broke out, the Orleans family fled to the safety of England. Shortly before they left Paris a picture was painted of the family, including Pamela, and hung in the Palace of Versailles.

In London, the brood was invited to spend a month as guests of Richard Brinsley Sheridan at Isleworth. The great Irish dramatist was then at the peak of his brilliance and popularity. Before the visit was over Sheridan and Pamela were engaged. However, the match was later broken off without explanation.

One night at the theatre the nineteen-year-old beauty was seen by Lord Edward Fitzgerald, who had gone to attend a performance of the play *Lodoiska*. He saw Pamela sitting in a box and sought an introduction when the curtain fell. The handsome Irish lord was immediately enslaved by her charm and they were married in less than a month, at Tourney, with the future king of France as one of the witnesses. They arrived in Dublin in February, 1793, and the woman born in a Fogo tilt dominated Irish society from the great Fitzgerald mansion, Leinster House.

Following her husband's death in the abortive uprising of 1798, Lady Fitzgerald resided in Germany with Madame de Genlis and married a United States consul, Mr. Pitcairn, in 1800. The marriage failed, so she divorced him and went to live in France under the name of Fitzgerald. She was completely ignored by the Orleans family. Her health, like her fortunes, took a downward turn. She died in a Paris convent at the age of fifty-five, November 9, 1831, and was buried at Montmartre. In 1880, her husband's family removed her bones to the Fitzgerald family vault near London. Part of the original tombstone, damaged in the siege of Paris, is incorporated in the memorial which now marks her grave.

In 1972, when I was doing research in Scotland for a history of St. John's, I spent several days going through the personal papers of the former Newfoundland governor, Sir Thomas Cochrane, which are in the National Library, Edinburgh. Buried in the papers I found a letter to His Excellency from John Chapman, Episcopal Missionary at Twillingate, dated 1836. The clergyman wrote, "In Christopher Ayre's letter to me, written by your direction in August 1834, relative to the birth of a child at Fogo, supposed to have become the wife of Lord Edward Fitzgerald, came to hand in October following...." Chapman went on to say that he sent a report of his investigations to the Governor but that, due to the neglect of the person to whom he committed them, George Stoneman of St. John's, they were not delivered. Fortunately, he kept a duplicate copy which he was forwarding to Cochrane. He adds:

> The two persons from whom I have collected the information contained are both living in Fogo now, and their statements are exactly the same as those of all the old inhabitants about Fogo, who remember anything about Nancy Syms and her child, which many of them do to this day. On my mind there is no

doubt but Nancy Syms child Ann was the very person who was taken with her mother to Christ Church. This far the history is quite clear, and I have no doubt but if the history of that child can be traced from that point, it will then appear quite evident that the same child afterwards became Lady Fitzgerald."

I could not find the duplicate copy with the Cochrane papers.

However, if further proof of Pamela's true identity is needed, Victor Hugo indicates she could have been adopted by Madame de Genlis. The birth certificate used at the time of her marriage to Lord Edward certainly identifies her as a native of Fogo, Newfoundland. The Fitzgerald family, on the other hand, has steadfastly denied what appears to be the origins of Lady Pamela.

Chapter Ten

Who Done It? Newfoundland's Unsolved Murders

Murder is not a criminal's crime. The majority of those who kill are very ordinary people and their action is one anybody can commit. However, we are not fascinated by murderers because they are like the rest of us, but because, in one respect, they are utterly different. In a moment of crisis they lack an instinct against killing, regardless of morality or deterrents. Slashed throats and indented skulls have no fascination in themselves. It is what has gone on in the mind of the man or woman who slashed the throat or dented the skull that draws the public to a study of crime.

In the unsolved crime, murder seems to show its most savage face. It is a tale without any real start. Usually we begin with a murder and work backwards from it, considering the evidence bearing on the crime, until we reach the beginning which is the solution. But in an unsolved crime, there is no starting point, only the grim ending, and we are left with a feeling of frustration at the impotence of justice. Newfoundland has had its share of such murders.

Between eleven o'clock and midnight Tuesday, October 2, 1855, a scuffle broke out on Water Street opposite McMurdo's Lane. There was no street lighting at the time, so passers-by were unable to distinguish the combatants. Suddenly, one of them slumped to the street. A lantern was fetched and it showed that a respectable 20-year-old, Dennis Summers, was dead in the gutter with a knife through his heart. Suspicion fell on several people but no charges were laid. The coroner's jury returned a verdict of wilful murder against a person or persons unknown. The crime went unsolved and newspapers of the day clamoured for the creation of a night watch composed of sober, efficient men, who would protect the citizens of St. John's from crime after dark.

In 1857 the murderer of Summers was apparently identified but never named. December 7 the *Newfoundlander* reported: "We learn that a young man who died recently in Britain, acknowledged before his death that he was the person who stabbed Dennis Summers, in Water Street, about two years ago, the act terminating fatally. A rigid inquiry was made at the time, and three men were detained on suspicion for some weeks, and subsequently released. The man who struck the blow was not one of these three, but one of the witnesses examined. We believe, however, that there was no premeditated ill-will connected with the unhappy case."

A celebrated murder that led to the banning of Christmas mummering in Newfoundland occurred at Bay Roberts in 1860. It also contributed to serious religious strife in Conception Bay. After dark on the evening of Friday, December 28, Thomas Mercer (often wrongly identified as Isaac Mercer), a young man who had been married two weeks before, was on his way back from work in the woods with two brothers-in-law when they called at his mother-in-law's house for a cup of tea. The trio then left for Mercer's home. At a turning in the road they were pounced upon by six mummers, who jumped from a hiding place and beat the three with sticks before fleeing into the darkness. Mercer was carried home by his companions. He said to his mother, "Oh mother, I am killed," and fell unconscious. Next day he passed away from a skull fracture. It was immediately said that the three Protestants were set upon by Roman Catholics and this led to religious riots all along the shore, seriously involving Bishop Feild in the controversy. Six names were freely mentioned in Bay Roberts. These men were examined but dismissed for lack of evidence.

A reward of £100 was offered to no effect. The coroner's verdict was "Wilful Murder". After the Attorney General returned to St.John's without discovering the murderers, a magistrate was sent to follow-up, but he found no new evidence. Because of the murder and religious disturbances, the Legislative Assembly passed an Act, June 25, 1861, making it illegal for any person in Newfoundland to go as a mummer, wearing a mask or otherwise disguised, unless licenced by a magistrate. The Act, which was often ignored but never repealed, gradually diminished the sport of Christmas mumming in the colony.

What is probably the most famous unsolved crime in local annals began on the evening of Wednesday, January 5, 1870, when 16-year old Elfrida Pike of Bristol's Hope was brutally murdered on the high road between Harbour Grace and Bristol's Hope, then called Mosquito. At six o'clock, the girl called at Mr. Parson's shop in Harbour Grace and purchased a small quantity of blue and some matches, afterwards found in the pocket of her dress.

Between half past six and seven, she was seen leaving Harbour Grace on the road home in the company of an unidentified young man. The winter's night was mild and bright, but about nine o'clock the wind veered north and there were some snow showers. The murder was not discovered until next morning, when a woman who was following behind her husband on the way home from chapel, noticed a pool of blood in the roadway beneath the melting snow. She glanced off the highroad and began to scream. Her husband ran back to find the lifeless body of the girl and hastened to the Magistrate.

Although young, the corpse was that of a fully developed woman of medium height and dark complexion. She is described as having a "kind, happy eye and smiling face, pleasing looking, if not pretty". Her moral character was said "to be free from stain" and on the evidence of a medical examination her remains were found "pure and unsullied". The girl had died from eight heavy blows of some blunt instrument, such as a stone. The head wounds alone were sufficient to destroy life. They appear to have been inflicted on the side of the road. The girl fell or crawled to the centre of the roadway, where her throat was cut from ear to ear. It looked as if the intent had been to sever the head. The body was then dragged to the opposite side of the road and left behind a large stone where it lay unseen by several passers-by. The time of death was estimated by the fact that her hat, which was covered by snow, rested on dry grass.

Mr. Mitchell, Superintendent of Police, was promptly dispatched to Harbour Grace and had two men taken up on suspicion. First one was released and then the other. Some 15 or 16 depositions were taken without throwing any light on the crime. The criminal must have been drenched in blood but he was never seen. A young female acquaintance who was with Elfrida on the evening of her murder, became suddenly and violently hysterical when questioned and remained in that state for many hours.

A large concourse of relatives, friends and the curious followed the girl to her grave when she was buried from the residence of her grandmother in Bear's Cove. The government offered a reward of $1,000, later increased to $1,200. An additional $400 was placed in the hands of Inspector Mitchell to be employed in obtaining secret information. The newspaper, *Telegraph* cried: "Justice would best be satisfied were the fiend to be subjected to the regular process of trial and then to be executed on the spot where he so brutally murdered his innocent victim". However, justice was not satisfied, and after more than 100 years it is unlikely we will ever learn the identity of the apparently motiveless murderer of Elfrida Pike.

The next unsolved murder in Newfoundland seems to have resulted from a fist fight. On the night of December 1, 1874, a young man named Peter Angel was involved in a fight in one of the dark lanes of Petty Harbour. He did not return home that Tuesday evening and was still missing next day, when his body was found floating in the harbour. The circumstances in which it was found gave rise to suspicion that his death was caused by violence greater than that inflicted in the fist fight. The Coroner and Inspector of Police with some of his men were sent to Petty Harbour to hold an inquest and take whatever steps were necessary. While it appeared a murder had been committed, no arrests were ever made.

Shortly afterwards attention was diverted from the Angel case by Newfoundland's greatest mass murder, a mystery that was never solved. On the evening of Sunday, December 20, 1874, the schooner *Grapeshot* was driven ashore in a gale and lost near Kingscove Head, Bonne Bay. She had on board a crew of six men and some 1,500 quintals of codfish. The owner, Edwin Duder, announced the loss of the vessel and added the good news that all hands were saved. Captain Rideout, the master, decided to walk overland to St. Georges where he and his crew could get passage to St. John's. The following year news reached the city that all six men had been found murdered. It was thought this was done by some person or persons employed to guide them to St. George's, but no charges were ever laid.

From the west coast we move to the south coast, where Burgeo became the scene of a celebrated unsolved homicide in 1876. John Bassett, alias Nelson (by the latter name he was generally known) was for many years a wharfinger of Messers De Quetteville and is said to have been esteemed by his employers. He was 62 years of age, very tall, well-made, and a heavy man. He was reputed to be strict with fishermen and servants and somewhat hot-tempered. Several threats had been made on his life.

For four or five Sundays he had been accustomed to walk after tea along the road leading to Upper Burgeo and at half-past seven on Sunday, August 13, 1876, he left three men with whom he had been chatting, to take his walk. A few minutes later he was seen about a half a mile distant by two girls, but was not seen again. A search was made on Monday and Tuesday in vain. On Wednesday afternoon, two women saw him floating in a pond some distance from the road. When the body was towed to shore by a fishing line it was found to have been savagely beaten. Severe blows had broken his nose, jaws, teeth, and arms. A sou'wester was fastened tightly under his chin by a sailor knot. His pockets were filled with stones and a rock was tied firmly to his left wrist with his own silk handkerchief. The body was very swollen and the skin looked as if it had been scorched and was ready to peel off. His clothes were strangely rotten but quite untorn, and his feet had on them the slippers he had walked in. It seems he had been carried, not dragged, from the road, and this feat would have taken two or three strong men. Several people who had uttered threats against the deceased in the past were questioned, but no arrests were ever made.

The first sensation of 1894 was the murder in St. John's of a junk dealer named William McCarthy, an old and feeble eccentric, who lived in a dilapidated shanty called Brass Castle on Springdale Street. His body, cold in death, was found at 10:30 on the evening of January 29th by a woman who entered his shop, saw blood around and called the police. The head appeared to have been smashed in with a 2½ foot long piece of gas pipe. Patrick Carrigan was held for questioning, but released when he proved he had been in the West End fire hall all evening. A Mrs. Jewer, who told a little girl from New Gower Street the news of McCarthy's death at 7:00 o'clock, was also taken for questioning but later released. When stains said to resemble blood were found on Carrigan's clothes he was picked up again and held for several days, but his alibi was air tight. By February 8th the *Evening Telegram* reported, "The sad affair has, so-to-speak, died out." The newspaper was right and the crime was soon forgotten.

One of the most puzzling unsolved murders in Newfoundland was discovered September 21, 1907, when the headless body of a man was found at Gull Marsh, Bonne Bay. The body measured 5'2" and there were two holes in the chest three inches beneath the collarbone. The clothes and singlet were spotted with blood. Police supposed it to have been thrown over a bridge and that it floated down to Gull Marsh. The head was never located and nobody was reported missing. Both victim and murderer went unidentified.

In more recent times, two suspected murders and one very brutal slaying involving females have joined the list of Newfoundland's unsolved crimes. On Monday, June 4, 1979, it was announced by the RCMP that wildlife officers, checking out a report on the weekend that there was an injured moose in the woods near the Trans Canada Highway, about 12 miles west of Corner Brook, had come upon the badly decomposed body of a woman thought to be in her late teens or early twenties.

The remains were flown to St. John's for an autopsy. On Wednesday she was revealed to be Janet Louvelle of 6 Juniper Terrace in Corner Brook. Her parents, Gordon and Josephine Louvelle, reported she had been missing since early February.

The seventeen-year-old girl was buried at 9:00 a.m. on Thursday from Holy Redeemer Cathedral. It was a long time before the results of the autopsy were made known and by then the case was almost forgotten by the public. No clues to any suspect in her death were ever found.

At 5:00 p.m., Monday, December 14, 1981, Donna Bradley, a pretty, fourteen-year-old student at I.J. Sampson School in St. John's telephoned her mother, Dawn Bradley, of 160 Patrick Street, to say she was leaving a friend's house on Currie Place, off Topsail Road, and was on her way home to supper. Her father was away working in Labrador.

A few minutes after the telephone call the girl left her friend's house and headed for the bus stop on the south side of Topsail Road, just east of Cowan Avenue, intending to stop at K Mart on the way and buy a card for her mother's birthday. She never reached home. On Wednesday her photograph appeared in the newspapers with the information that she was missing and police were concerned for her safety. Detective Lloyd Ford said the matter was being taken more seriously than most missing person reports. She was known to hitch hike and anyone having seen a person of her description getting into a car, or boarding a bus, was asked to contact the police.

Some witnesses came forward to say they saw her entering a car at the bus stop about 5:20 Monday. The driver was thought to be a man in his mid-twenties of average height and weight, with light brown, medium length, unkempt hair. He was clean shaven. The car was described as a 1973 to 1976 four-door Dodge Dart or Plymouth Valiant of a beige, tan or faded yellow colour with rust marks on the lower body. These details relating to both the driver and the car seem remarkable in view of the fact that the five-foot-five 110-pound hitch hiker was picked up in the darkness of late afternoon in mid-December.

Around three o'clock on Friday Dale Smith of Shea Heights, and his wife Helen, decided to take their three young children with them to search for a Christmas tree before dark. They parked on the Maddox Cove Road, just west of where it turns into the Cape Spear Road, and started down a small path into the woods. They went only a short distance before they

71

stumbled upon the battered body of a dead girl. Sensing that it was probably the bludgeoned corpse of Donna Bradley they ran back to their car to go for help. Just down the road they met a man, told him what had happened, brought him to the foot path and asked him to stand guard while they went to the police.

In a very short time the area was closed off by the RCMP and a tracking dog scoured the nearby woods without result. About 7:00 o'clock in the evening the remains were removed to the city morgue. On Monday the police released a rather crude composite drawing said to resemble the man who picked up the girl in his car. A 20-man team investigated the flood of leads that were telephoned in to the RCMP and a search of thousands of motor registration files lead to hundreds of interviews with car owners. Some people were taken in for questioning, but no arrest warrant was ever issued.

On Monday afternoon, December 21, the Christmas spirit was muted in St. John's as the slain girl's mother, father, grade nine classmates and many hundreds of the morbidly curious crowded Wesley United Church and lined Patrick Street for the funeral. Reverend Robert Mills urged family and friends not to dwell "on the pain, the savagery and the anger" but to turn toward their faith in God. Emotions ran high among the young people during the internment at Mount Pleasant Cemetery.

After Christmas police were saying there was essentially nothing new to report. Some witnesses were out of town because of the holidays and, on their return, a more detailed drawing of the suspect was promised. On the 30th the new composite, based on the descriptions of two witnesses was released to the media. It showed a pleasant young man with tousled hair framing a not unattractive face. However, the numerous telephone calls it produced brought no result.

There were two minor sensations connected with the case. Excitement gripped the public when the police asked for information about a man seen hovering in the woods near where the corpse was found for some hours on the afternoon before the discovery of the body by the Smith family. Nobody seemed able to provide any clue as to his identity.

A rumour circulated through the city like wildfire that the

body of a second female had been found in the same area as that of the Bradley girl. There was much speculation that it might be Sharon Drover, a seventeen-year-old who left her home on Livingstone Street on the evening of December 29, 1978, to go to work at McDonald's Restaurant on Kenmount Road and was never seen again. However, Inspector John Lavers of the RCMP who was heading a team of seventeen Mounted Police and three detectives of the Royal Newfoundland Constabulary's Criminal Investigation Division, denied the rumours.

By the end of January the murder probe was broadened to include the whole of the Avalon Peninsula and later extended to the cars of Newfoundlanders who had gone to work in the oil fields of Alberta. Days passed and other events caught the attention of the media and the imagination of the public. Finally it was announced that the investigating team was being disbanded. The Ocean Ranger oil rig tragedy in March 1981 swept the Bradley case from memory. It is certain to take its place as one of the great unsolved murders in Newfoundland criminal history.

This list is by no means complete. It merely sets down some of the interesting unsolved murders I have discovered in doing research. For every solved homicide in Newfoundland, as elsewhere, I am sure there is an undetected one, proving that in some instances crime does seem to pay.

Chapter Eleven

Humphrey Gilbert and the Birth of an Empire

Sir Humphrey Gilbert was the elder half-brother of Sir Walter Raleigh. It was Sir Walter who reputedly threw his cape in the mud to keep Queen Elizabeth's feet dry as she stepped from her coach. When Gilbert's father died his mother married a second time. She was a good woman who sent all her boys to the best schools and later to university.

In 1563, Humphrey Gilbert was at Havre in France where he heard tales of the attempts at settlement along the St. Lawrence River in the New World by Jacques Cartier and Roberval. Their deeds fired his nationalistic spirit and, in 1566, he showed himself a champion of English expansion by publishing *Discourse Of A Discovery For A New Passage To Cataia*. His thoughts were of an ocean voyage to the west and he gave himself up to the study of geography, navigation and the history of discovery.

Gilbert believed there existed a northwest passage to the Indies and Japan. He petitioned the queen in May 1565, stating that "there is no doubt of a passage to be found." He offered to undertake a journey of discovery with his brothers at their own expense, so long as they were granted certain rights and trading monopolies. Sir Humphrey wrote to his brother, John, that a passage to China existed "through a sea which lieth on the Northside of Labrador."

Although Gilbert's *Discourse* gave voice to what was being said by a small circle of scholars and sailors about English sea policy, the oldest brother, John, answered that the proposed voyage "seemed strange and had not been commonly spoken of before." In July 1566, there were serious uprisings in Ireland and all thoughts of a sea journey had to be abandoned. Shane O'Neill had raised the banners of rebellion in Ulster and all Ireland was aflame. England answered with a campaign of terror and colonization. During the next four years, Gilbert practiced habitual bestiality in Ireland as he tried to make the name of Englishmen "more terrible now to them than the sight of a hundred was before." While his conduct of the warfare in Ulster, and later as colonel in command of the forces in Munster, won acclaim from the government in England, he wrote to a friend that it would "in the end turn to my utter confusion and discredit, rather than to increase my poor reputation."

By efficient, cruel and savage butchery he laid waste to Ireland and filled the hearts of the Irish people with dread and fear. It was said that Irishmen of the time "looked like anatomies of death; they spoke like ghosts crying out of their graves; they did eat the dead carrions, happy when they would find them; yea they did eat one another soon after, inasmuch as the very carcasses they spared not to drag out of their graves." For having done this the Lord Deputy wrote: "I had nothing to present him with but the honour of knighthood, which I gave him." His half-brother, Raleigh, had written from Munster of Sir Humphrey, "I have never heard or read of any man more feared than he is among the Irish nation."

In 1567 Humphrey Gilbert had begun looking among his Devonshire friends for partners in a plantation venture in Ulster, but when duty took him to Munster, he transferred his hopes for a settlement to some land that two west of England adventurers bought from the Desmond family around Baltimore in the county of Cork. A town was to be built at Baltimore and a country established with "English birth and government" which would replace the rebel Irish and become a little England on which the backers would grow fabulously rich. The dream vanished with the eruption of James FitzMaurice's rebellion in Munster. Instead of a wealthy plantation owner, Gilbert became the scourge of Ireland as he put the devastated land to the torch and sword.

In January 1570 Gilbert left Ireland and returned to England, being owed the sum of £3315. Two years later, he wrote his uncle that he was again trying to found a colony in County Cork but lacked finances. In 1571 he entered Parliament, having been elected for the town of Plymouth. The poet, George

Gascoigne, visited him at his home in Limehouse in 1575 and found him at work on various schemes of colonization. In August 1577 it was rumoured that Gilbert was ready to sail to Peru, but he needed the queen's permission to make the voyage. In November he asked Elizabeth if he might fit out an expedition to seize and despoil the Newfoundland fishing fleets of Spain, Portugal and France, creep down the coast of America for an assault on the Spanish Indies, take Santo Domingo and Cuba and make them English colonies and bases for the destruction of the Spanish empire.

The plan proved too bold and probably too expensive for the queen and the concept was abandoned by delay and indecision. Sir Humphrey redrew his proposals towards colonization and on June 11, 1578, the queen granted him letters patent "to discover search find out and view such remote heathen and barbarous lands countries and territories not actually possessed by any Christian prince or people." He was given six years in which to carry out the task and the lands he found were his "to have hold occupy and enjoy...forever." He would legislate and administer the colony as a vassal of the English crown. No reasons were given for the colony, nor was any site mentioned, although his destination was thought to be somewhere south of the Hudson River.

Once given a licence to satisfy their obscure desires, Gilbert and his partners began to quarrel. Henry Knollys refused to accept a subordinate position and left in his ship, *Francis*, taking two others with him. The captains of most of the other vessels were well-known pirates. September 26th a fleet of eleven ships and 500 men sailed from Dartmouth, only to be driven back to shore by contrary winds. A second attempt was made in October with the same result. On November 18th after much argument, ill-will and recrimination, three more of the vessels turned to piracy and sailed off in search of plunder. Gilbert, in command of the *Anne Aucher,* departed England the next day with six ships carrying 409 men. One of these vessels, the queen's ship, *Falcon*, was captained by Sir Walter Raleigh. Storms, greed and ambition soon dispersed the fleet and by April, 1579, Gilbert was home in England, claiming "a great loss because I would not myself, nor suffer any of my company to do anything contrary to my word given to her Majesty."

In June of that year, he was back in Ireland trying to subdue the renewed threat of James FitzMaurice. This service cost him dearly, for his sailors took off with two of his best ships, leaving him with only the little *Squirrel*, a frigate of less than ten tons. To re-establish his fortune he decided to exploit his patent of 1578. He sold or mortgaged his property to raise new funds. This time it was his intention to plant and fortify a colony somewhere in the warm lands of the New World, perhaps as far south as Florida.

Those who dismissed him as a dreamer in 1566 were hungry to invest in settling the distant lands by 1580, and there was much support for the venture. Two of the backers were English Catholic gentlemen. A government agent reported April 19, 1582, "there is a muttering among Papists that Sir Humphry Gilbert goeth to seek a new found land, Sir George Peckham and Sir Thomas Gerrard goeth with him." Gilbert assigned over 8 million acres of his new colony to the Catholics and another 3 million to Sir Philip Sidney. Peckham and Gerrard saw hope of practicing their faith without becoming enemies of their country in the new colony. 1581 had been a hard year on Catholics in England, with severe penalties enacted against them and the execution of the Jesuit, Edmund Campion.

It was hoped to have the expedition sail before the end of 1582, but the departure was delayed by worries about finance. Partners and plans changed as backers came and went. Elizabeth began to have second thoughts about the venture and early in 1583 sent word to Gilbert that he was not to accompany the expedition. She considered him a man "of not good happ by sea." However, in a spirited appeal, he convinced the queen to change her mind.

By mid-March the expedition was ready to sail. Stephen Parmenius, a young Hungarian poet, wrote an embarkation ode of 300 Latin hexameters and joined the company, possibly as secretary to Sir Humphrey. Five ships gathered at Causand Bay near Plymouth. Gilbert commanded from the *Delight* (120 tons). Sir Walter Raleigh's was the largest ship, the barque

Raleigh (200 tons), but he remained at home because of illness. The *Golden Hind* was owned by Edward Hayes, who was to become the historian of the venture. The *Swallow* (40 tons) was an ex-pirate vessel captured by Gilbert and there was his own ship of many years, the *Squirrel*. There were 260 men including shipwrights, masons, carpenters, smiths, mineral men and refiners. For their entertainment and solace there were musicians and clowns.

The fleet departed England June 11th, "the weather and wind fair and good all day, but a great storm of thunder and wind fell the same night." Newfoundland was the closest landfall where stores could be replenished from fishermen's supplies, so they sought "the trade way unto Newfoundland," intending to then proceed south without delay. Only two days out, the barque *Raleigh* turned back to port. The reason is obscure and appears to have been either sickness breaking out or a fear among the crew of a lack of victuals. The remaining ships lost each other in a fog. Seven weeks out from England, steep cliffs rose out of the mist and haze. The *Delight* and the *Golden Hind* sailed south along the Newfoundland coast and came upon the *Swallow* in Conception Bay. Meeting a solitary fishing vessel, her crew had taken to piracy. Gilbert was angered but could do little. Later that day they met the *Squirrel* at anchor near the mouth of St. John's harbour.

Seeing four strange vessels suddenly appear, the fishermen of the place feared a pirate raid and opposed Gilbert's entry to the port until he produced his patent from the queen. August 3, 1583, Sir Humphrey sailed through the Narrows. His ship grounded on Pancake Rock and had to be hauled off. He was welcomed on shore by a small community of men from several nations who had built onshore habitations, works for the repair and support of their boats, and also planted simple crops of vegetables when they arrived in May, which they harvested before they left in August.

Monday, August 5th, Gilbert founded the British Empire when he went ashore at St. John's and took possession of Newfoundland in the name of Queen Elizabeth. He promulgated three laws, imposed taxes, demanded the revictualling of his ships, claimed possession of the harbour and two hundred leagues every way. The three laws, the first English rule proclaimed in the western world, stated that public worship was to be according to the Church of England, any attempt prejudicial to Her Majesty's right and possession of the territory was to be punished as in a case of high treason, and anyone uttering words of dishonour to Her Majesty should "lose his ears and have his ship and goods confiscate." He then erected "the Arms of England ingraven in lead, and infixed upon a pillar of wood." Sickness and desertion so undermanned the four ships that he took all the healthy crewmen and put the others aboard the *Swallow* to return to England, while he sailed south towards Nova Scotia. August 29th they ran into a storm and the *Delight* was lost with 200 men, including the poet, Stephen Parmenius. The weather was cold and windy and the coast full of dangers, so Gilbert was prevailed upon to abandon the voyage and return to England. He promised to borrow £10,000 from Her Majesty and set forth royally the next spring to settle a colony in Newfoundland, claiming "I am now become a northern man altogether, and my heart is set on Newfoundland." The fact was he had no choice, as his patent was about to expire, leaving him only those lands he had already claimed.

On the voyage home to England Gilbert stupidly and stubbornly sailed in the little *Squirrel*. September 9th the fleet ran into a storm. Edward Hayes writes, "In the afternoon the frigate was neere cast away....the General sitting abaft with a book in his hands, cried out unto us in the *Hind*...we are as neere to heaven by sea as by land." Sir Humphrey proved to be nearer to heaven (or hell) by sea than he thought, for about twelve o'clock that night, according to Hayes, "the frigate was devoured and swallowed up by the sea." With Gilbert died Newfoundland's great opportunity to become the first important colony. The later ventures of men such as John Guy and Lord Baltimore were nothing compared to the vision of Sir Humphrey Gilbert.

Chapter Twelve

The Trans-Atlantic Cable To Heart's Content

It is a delight to find the old cable offices in Heart's Content turned into one of the best set up and most interesting museums in Atlantic Canada. Because of the daring enterprise of Cyrus Field, which after many disappointments reached its hour of triumph, the settlement was given a place in the history of world communications.

The community is first mentioned by John Guy in 1612 and is thought to have been named after a ship. We know that in Guy's time there were ships in England with such names as Heart's Ease, Heart's Desire, Heart's Content, etc. The *Heart's Ease* voyaged to the west coast of Greenland in 1612. John Mason, a governor of Guy's colony, captured a Sallee pirate, the *Heart's Desire*, in Ireland in 1625. It seems more than likely Heart's Content was called after the English vessel of the same name.

The first suggestion to link Europe to North America by a cable from Ireland to Newfoundland was made by Bishop Mullock in a letter he wrote November 8, 1850, to the editor of the *Courier*, a St. John's newspaper. This was followed by a visit to Newfoundland in the spring of 1851 by Frederick Gisborne, who proposed to the Legislature the laying of a cable to connect Newfoundland to Nova Scotia. A local company was organized and, after raising the necessary funds, work was begun on the project in 1853.

The following year Gisborne was in New York where he met a young man named Cyrus Field, a wealthy merchant who had retired from business the previous year. After hearing Gisborne talk of his telegraph linking Newfoundland with the rest of North America, it occurred to Field that a cable might be laid to span the Atlantic Ocean. He contacted Professor Morse to see if a telegraph signal could cover such a great distance. Encouraged by the inventor of morse code, Field set out to lay an Atlantic cable.

The project, begun in 1854, did not get underway until 1858. There were many setbacks and disappointments. Gisborne's first attempt to lay a cable from Newfoundland to Nova Scotia in 1855 ended in failure. A second attempt, in 1856, was successful. The following year the British Navy mapped the bed of the Atlantic Ocean. Cyrus Field's project was funded and a company organized. The contract for the cable was signed. Field had to go to Washington to fight opposition in Congress to his wasting funds on an impossible scheme. By early 1857 the enterprise was ready to get underway as a joint British-U.S. venture, with both governments cooperating in the charter of naval ships.

The first attempt to lay an Atlantic cable was made in the summer of 1857. As there was no single ship afloat large enough to hold the vast coil of wire needed to link Europe to North America, it was decided to lay it from two vessels. The British Government lent the HMS *Agamemnon* and the United States Government the USS *Niagara*. On August 5th, they met at Valentia, an island off County Kerry, Ireland. The Lord Lieutenant of Ireland, the Earl of Carlyle, bestowed his blessings on the expedition and the operation got underway. The short end of the cable was brought to land by one of *Niagara*'s boats. She was to lay the first half from Ireland to the middle of the Atlantic. The end would then be spliced to the other half on board *Agamemnon*. That night a banquet was given by the Knight of Kerry and a ball was held, which continued until dawn.

The following morning the *Niagara* began laying cable on the ocean bed, but after only five miles it snapped. It was recovered and spliced. By August 11th (4 days out), 380 miles of cable had been put down when a mechanic applied the brake too hard and the cable once more parted. Efforts to recover it were fruitless and the expedition had to be abandoned, as it was too late in the year to begin again. This ended the first attempt to lay an Atlantic cable. About $250,000 was lost on the scheme.

A second attempt was made the following year. This time

the two ships were to meet in mid-ocean, splice the cable and begin laying it in opposite directions. On June 10, 1858, the two ends of the coil were joined and the vessels began to steam apart, one to the east and the other to the west. When some 200 miles had been laid, the cable broke once more and the fault could not be repaired immediately. The vessels returned to Ireland. Having re-supplied, they set sail a second time to retrieve the lost cable from the ocean bottom and continue the project. It was raised and spliced on July 29th. The rest of the voyage was strangely uneventful.

The *Niagara* landed her end of the cable at Bay Bulls Arm, Trinity Bay, Newfoundland, August 15, 1858. It was carried to a building erected above the shore and connected to the electrical equipment. That same day the *Agamemnon* reached Valentia, Ireland, and at 6 a.m. the European end of the cable was brought ashore. By 3 p.m. it was taken into the electrical room and attached to a galvanometer. Shortly afterwards, the first instant messages were transmitted from the old world to the new. In New York there were torchlight processions and in England a knighthood was conferred on George Bright, the 26-year-old British engineer in charge of the operation. Cyrus Field, because he was an American, could only receive the congratulations of the Queen. The first messages were an exchange between Victoria and President Buchanan. It took 10 hours for the cable from London to reach Washington because the undersea connection between Newfoundland and Nova Scotia was out of order. Messages had to be carried across Cabot Strait by the steamship *Victoria*.

Dr. Whitestone and Professor Thompson, two of the scientists involved in the enterprise, engaged in a controversy about how much voltage should be applied to the cable. Unfortunately, Whitestone won the argument and a higher voltage than Thompson wanted was applied. It was too much. Within two hours the cable began to fail. It soon became necessary to repeat each message six times. The rate charged was $100 for a minimum of 20 words. By September the link was so bad that only a few words could be transmitted at intervals, and on October 20th it went completely dead. The Atlantic

82

Telegraph Company had to face the fact that it had lost a further $2,500,000 of its capital. The returns consisted of receipts from August 16th to October 20th and they were very small. Some money was made by Cyrus Field, who sold surplus cable to the New York jewellers, Tiffany's, who cut it in 6-inch lengths, mounted them in silver and sold them as souvenirs, with a facsimile of a certificate signed by Field as proof of their origin.

Attempts by Field to revive the company met with profound discouragement. Many people voiced doubts that the cable had ever worked. The outbreak of Civil War in America in September 1861 put an end to all hope of renewing the project.

In 1864 Cyrus Field began new efforts to lay a greatly improved Atlantic cable at an estimated cost of $2,500,000. This time it was decided to use one ship and the choice was the *Great Eastern* — a vessel six times the size of any ship then afloat. It would be 40 years before the world would see her like again. On launching she was named *Leviathan* but was registered as *Great Eastern*. She was fully rigged as a sailing ship, with 6 masts, a pair of steam-powered paddle wheels and a screw propeller. She was the first great ship of the modern age and, because she was before her time, she has been described as a magnificent failure. The owners offered use of *Great Eastern* to lay the cable. If successful in the attempt, they were to receive approximately $100,000 in the company's stock. If it failed they were to get nothing. The proposition appealed to Field.

July 23, 1865, *Great Eastern* put out to sea from Valentia, Ireland. On August 2nd, when two-thirds of the way across the Atlantic, (having laid out 1,186 miles) the cable parted without warning. An attempt was made to grapple the lost wires 12,000 feet below. At 6 a.m. on August 3rd the grapnel hooked the cable. At 2,800 feet the wire broke and the cable was lost a second time. The *Great Eastern* was forced to return to Valentia.

The undaunted Cyrus Field did not give up hope. He made immediate preparations for another attempt the following year. On Friday, July 13, 1866, the *Great Eastern* once more sailed from Ireland. This attempt proceeded almost without incident, and at 9 o'clock on the morning of July 27 the mighty vessel arrived at Heart's Content, Newfoundland. Later in the day sailors bore the end of the cable to shore. The excitement everywhere was tremendous. Sailors capered about as they stepped on dry land and newspapers tell us one even put the end of the cable in his mouth and sucked it like a lollipop. Church bells were rung and a small harmonium was brought to the shore in front of the present museum, where a "Te Deum" was sung. Messages were exchanged between Queen Victoria and President Andrew Johnson. Throughout August the *Great Eastern* attempted to retrieve the lost cable from the previous year. A little before 1 a.m. on September 2nd it was hoisted on board from the ocean floor. A splice was made and by 7 o'clock the great ship was steaming back to Newfoundland, laying out a second cable. On the evening of September 8th the end of this cable was also landed at Heart's Content. Two lines of communication now existed between Europe and North America. Knighthoods, banquets, medals, parades and eulogies followed and Cyrus Field was the hero of the age.

Captain Halpin, of *Great Eastern*, married a Newfoundland girl he met on the voyage — a Miss Munn, the daughter of a prominent Harbour Grace merchant family. They honeymooned on the voyage back to Britain. The huge ship was laid up for the next eleven years at Milford Haven in Wales. She was never put to sea again, but ended her days as a floating fun fair under charter to a Liverpool department store. Cyrus Field died in 1892. For some strange reason his genius has been almost forgotten by his countrymen.

Chapter Thirteen

Sir Wilfred Grenfell — Labrador's Man of Legend

In 1869 James Gordon Bennett, of the New York *Herald Tribune*, hired Henry Morton Stanley to "start looking round for Livingstone." The Scottish missionary doctor and explorer in Africa, who discovered Victoria Falls, had been long unheard from and was even thought dead. November 10, 1871, Stanley claims to have slashed his way through the trees at Ujiji and come upon a pale, weary-looking white man with grey whiskers and moustache, wearing a red-sleeved waistcoat and a pair of grey trousers. Not knowing quite what to do he walked deliberately up to him, took off his hat, and said, "Dr. Livingstone, I presume?" The old man answered with a kind smile, "Yes." Stanley reached civilization in May 1872 and caused a sensation throughout the world with news of the meeting at Ujiji.

One of those who undoubtedly heard with avid interest talk of Stanley's meeting with Livingstone, was a six-year-old schoolboy in England who would one day become almost as legendary a missionary doctor in North America as Livingstone had become in Africa. Wilfred Thomason Grenfell was born in Cheshire on February 28, 1865. Events were to make him the most impressive and controversial figure in the history of Northern Newfoundland and Labrador. After taking medical training at London University and London Hospital, he undertook the Superintendency of the Royal National Mission to Deep Sea Fishers in 1889. His work as a missionary doctor bears a resemblance to Livingstone's in that both men dedicated their lives to helping underprivileged natives in remote regions of two great continents.

In 1891 Mr. Francis Hopwood, the future Lord Southborough, and a member of the Mission board, returned to

85

England from a visit to Canada and Newfoundland and brought before members the opportunities for service among the fishermen of the northwest Atlantic, who were said to be in need of both spiritual and physical healing. One of those who volunteered to go was Wilfred Grenfell. Some said it was under strong religious excitement and in response to a deep-seated wish to be nearer to God that he volunteered. Grenfell himself claims in his autobiography that it was the venture itself which attracted him, and he went just because he wanted to.

In the spring of 1892 he set out for Newfoundland in a boat that was ketch-rigged, much like a yawl. Although himself a master mariner, he left the charge of the vessel to an experienced crew of North Sea fishermen. Their first sight of land was Cape St. Francis. As they neared St. John's in July, they could see dense columns of smoke arising and feel the shore wind growing hotter and hotter. When the pilot boat towed them through the Narrows, they were amazed to see a dozen fiercely raging fires burning among the ruins of what had been a city. It was the day after the Great Fire of 1892 which destroyed much of St. John's.

Dr. Grenfell had expected to spend most of his time cruising among fishing schooners on the Grand Banks, but he was advised it would be more profitable if he were to follow the large fleet of over one hundred banking schooners which had sailed North to Labrador in late spring, carrying some 30,000 men, women and children to the Northern fishery. He reached the Labrador Coast on the fourth of August and it was to prove his moment of destiny. Invited to come ashore and treat a very sick man, he entered a tiny sod-covered hovel which had a doorway and one window of broken glass. Six neglected and frightened children huddled in a corner. The sick man was coughing his soul out in the darkness of a bunk, while his pitiably clad wife gave him cold water to sip from a spoon. The man had pneumonia and was probably tubercular. There was little the doctor could do but pray for the man with his family, and hand out a few packages of medicine and food. When he called back a month later, the poor wretch was dead and buried and the family totally destitute. Wilfred Grenfell had lost his first patient, but the pattern of his life was changed and he was to devote the rest of his days to working among the people of Labrador and Northern Newfoundland, saving many thousands of lives that would otherwise have been lost.

After wintering in England, Grenfell returned to Labrador the following spring, accompanied by several volunteers. When the fishing season closed in the autumn, he decided not to go home immediately, but to visit Canada with an Australian colleague, Dr. Bobardt, and try to raise funds to carry on the mission work begun in Labrador. In Montreal Lord Strathcona presented the Mission with a fine little steamer. After touring Canada, the two doctors returned to England for the winter. Grenfell was back in Montreal in the spring and he took the little ship down the St. Lawrence and along the Straits to Battle Harbour. There he was greeted by doctors, nurses and supplies from England.

Sir Thomas Roddick, the great Montreal physician and a former Newfoundlander, presented Grenfell with a splendid twenty-foot jolly-boat, rigged with full sail and centre-boom and in this he cruised the Labrador. If he knew the people of the coast before, it was that summer he learned to love them. In the years which followed, his love was to find expression in many ways.

In response to letters from Newfoundland begging the Mission in London to establish a winter station at St. Anthony, Grenfell disembarked with real keenness at the northern community in sub-arctic November weather, rented a couple of rooms in the chief merchant's house and hired a former guide as dog-driver. Soon after his arrival on the Labrador Coast, the doctor had noticed that the Hudson Bay Company paid wages with tin money, stamped "Only valuable at our store". Such incidents led him to the belief that the people should be freed from the barter system, so he encouraged the establishment of the cooperative plan which had proven so successful in England. This made him enemies among the small traders as well as the big merchants. The first cooperative store opened at Red Bay 1896. Eventually there were ten such stores as far north as Battle Harbour.

The poverty which the doctor witnessed in Canada Bay, near St. Anthony, led to the establishment of a saw mill there, with the help of a special grant from the government. The Mission Board considered the venture outside their sphere and the whole expense was borne by Grenfell, who was advised he was undertaking more than he could handle, knowing nothing whatever of mills. When the saw mill was successfully established, the doctor turned his attention to breeding foxes for the market value of their skins. A fox farm was begun at St. Anthony.

The illiteracy and ignorance of Northern Newfoundland and Labrador was a great handicap to the people, and eventually Dr. Grenfell aspired to build Mission Schools. He did not approve of the denominational system of education and this brought him into conflict with the leaders of several religious bodies in St. John's. He felt that the presence of inadequate schools of three or four denominations in a single community was needless duplication, a waste of money, and of little value to the students. He fought for a free public school at St. Anthony. It was begun in a small way and, as it grew, children were brought in as boarders from the northern district. Many young people were introduced to such childhood games as "Ring-around-Rosie" and "The Farmer in the Dell' for the first time at the schools the doctor opened. With the cooperation of the teachers, and gifts from friends in the United States, libraries were established.

After much agitation on Grenfell's part, the Government of Newfoundland constructed the first of several lighthouses along the Labrador coast, and these were of great benefit to him in visiting the hospitals he soon established at Battle Harbour, Harrington, Indian Harbour and North West River. He also built nursing stations at Flower's Cove, Forteau, Mutton Bay, St. Mary's River, Spotted Islands and Batteau.

Besides the school at St. Anthony, there was an orphanage as well. Schools and orphanages were also completed at North West River and Cartwright. He built a school only at St. Mary's River.

Experiments with caribou led the doctor to decide on the importation of reindeer from Lapland. Around 300 animals were purchased and three Lapp families were hired and brought from Finland to teach the local people how to herd the animals. The deer adapted well to life in their new country, but the Lapps suffered from homesickness and the cold. Finally they went back to Lapland and, with nobody to supervise the herding, the deer herd began to decline as poaching increased at an alarming rate. Killing of the animals was soon made legal in certain areas and, within a short time the promising experiment ended with the shipment of the remaining animals to Canada.

One of Dr. Grenfell's most exciting adventures, and one which became the subject of a book, began Easter Sunday, April 21, 1908, which was still winter in Northern Newfoundland. The doctor was called from Easter Sunday morning services at St. Anthony to treat a boy with a badly infected leg at Brent's Island, sixty miles to the south.

Grenfell, who was then 43, harnessed seven huskies and, taking his pet spaniel, Jack, with him, covered 20 miles before nightfall. Next morning he unwisely decided to chance a short cut across 10 miles of frozen sea. The ice in the bay already showed signs of spring break-up and it was a gamble. When he was halfway across, there was a wind change and the ice began moving off-shore. The doctor removed his heavy oil skins and shouted to the dogs to make a quick dash to land, but it was too late. The komotik fell through loose ice and Grenfell just had time to slash the dogs free of the harness before the sled sank with his supplies. He clung to the lead dog's thong as the huskies floundered in the water and eventually coaxed the animals onto an ice pan about 10 feet square.

Soaked and freezing, he cut his high boots at the ankles and made a leather wind break for his back. He realized survival depended on his remaining calm. Then he made a decision which haunted him for the rest of his life. He knew some of the dogs had to be killed if he was to survive. With a surgeon's precision he plunged the knife into three of the animals, being bitten twice, skinned them for their shaggy furs, and made a wind-break of their bodies.

By nightfall, Grenfell was ten miles from shore and drifting further out to sea. Fortunately, the wind died down and the temperature stayed at 27°F above zero. Using the frozen legs of the dogs, he made a sort of pole to which he attached his shirt in hopes it might be sighted by someone.

Unknown to the doctor, watchers on land had seen his distress after first mistaking him for a floating log. However, it was too close to darkness to send out a boat. Grenfell was long overdue at the village and everyone wondered if the figure on the ice-pan could be him. In the morning five men launched a boat and, by rowing it in the open water and climbing out to drag it over numerous ice-pans, they eventually reached the doctor, who was a grotesque, half-frozen figure, huddled in the bloodstained skins of the dead dogs.

When he reached shore Grenfell recovered enough to visit the sick boy. He amputated the infected leg and saved the lad's life. He later erected a plaque to the three huskies he had been forced to kill to ensure his own survival.

Sir Wilfred Grenfell's greatest contribution to life in Labrador and Northern Newfoundland was the chain of hospitals which he built. It began with the cottage hospitals at Battle Harbour and Indian River. They were opened in buildings donated by Baine Johnston & Company and Job Brothers, two St. John's mercantile firms with fishing interests in the communities. A few years later, a hospital was opened in a cottage at St. Anthony as a summer medical headquarters, but in time it became the focal point for Dr. Grenfell's work in the north. When a new eight-bed hospital was erected at St. Anthony in 1927, the project was directed by one of the Labrador orphans raised by the mission who had studied engineering in New York.

To support the doctor's work, admirers in the United States, Canada, and Great Britain formed the International Grenfell Association in 1912. It is still very active in overseeing projects in Newfoundland and Labrador.

A knighthood was conferred on Wilfred Grenfell in 1927. He retired as Superintendent of the I.G.A. Mission in 1937 at the age of 72. The following year, Lady Grenfell, an American socialite he met and married on an international cruise in 1908, died after a long and painful illness. The doctor made his last trip to St. Anthony to bury her ashes. October 9, 1940, he passed away while quietly sitting in a chair at his home on Lake Champlain in Vermont. In his time he had formed six hospitals, seven nursing stations, orphanage-boarding schools, cooperative stores, fourteen industrial centres, and a cooperative lumber mill. Arrogant, opinionated and domineering, intolerant of denominationalism, and bitter enemy of the exploitation of the impoverished working class people of Northern Newfoundland and Labrador, Sir Wilfred Grenfell found many enemies. He also found immortality.

An interesting but little known fact about Grenfell is that when he was preparing for the 1886 examinations of the Royal College of Physicians and the Royal College of Surgeons of England, he had as his hospital chief at the London Hospital in Whitechapel, Sir Frederick Treves. It was Treves who rescued Joseph Merrick, known to history as "The Elephant Man", from exploitation in a freak show. In recent years the story of Treves and Merrick has been the subject of several books, a highly acclaimed stage play and an award winning movie. One of the assignments the famous doctor gave his young house surgeon was to care for Merrick, who was suffering from an affliction which we know today to be friboneuromatosis.

In his biography, *A Labrador Doctor*, Grenfell writes:

It so happened that there was at that time in hospital under my care a patient known as 'the elephant man.' He had been starring under this title in a cheap vaudeville, had been seen by some of the students, and invited over to be shown to and studied by our best physicians. The poor fellow was really exceedingly sensitive about his most extraordinary appearance. The disease was called "leontiasis", and consisted of an enormous over-development of bone and skin on one side. His head and face were so deformed as really to resemble a big animals's head with a trunk. My arms would not reach around his hat. A special room in the yard was allotted to him, and several famous people came to see him — among them Queen Alexandra, then the Princess of Wales, who afterward sent him an autographed photograph of herself. He kept it in his room which was known as the 'elephant house,' and it always suggested beauty and the beast. Only at night

91

could the man venture out of doors, and it was no unusual thing in the dusk of nightfall to meet him walking up and down in the little courtyard. He used to talk freely of how he would look in a huge bottle of alcohol — an end to which in his imagination he was fated to come. He was of a very cheerful disposition and pathetically proud of his left side which was very normal. Very suddenly one day he died — the reason assigned being that his head fell forward and choked him, being too heavy for him to lift up.

Chapter Fourteen

The First Nuns in British North America

In 1833 there were two orders of English-speaking nuns in the United States. There were none at all in what was then called British North America, including Newfoundland. That spring Bishop Michael Anthony Fleming left St. John's for Ireland, feeling "the necessity of withdrawing female children from under the tutelage of men...." He was determined to bring back a congregation of Irish sisters to teach poor girls.

Dr. Fleming was a Waterford man whose search brought him to the door of the Presentation Convent in Galway City on the morning of June 29th, carrying his belongings in a carpet bag. Sister Magdelene O'Shaughnessey answered his knock. He introduced himself as an "American" bishop and asked permission to say mass. The young nun ran off and came back a few minutes later with Mother John Power's approval.

Perhaps it was after saying mass, during the breakfast the sisters served him, that he spoke to the Superior of his intention to seek volunteers for the Newfoundland mission. Mother John was in sympathy with his proposal and allowed him to address the congregation and outline his needs. While speaking in the most fervent tones about the desolation of his diocese, the bishop suddenly turned to Sister Magdelene, who was plying him with endless questions, and said, "You must come out with me to Newfoundland. There is the only way you can save your soul." She was the first of the congregation to volunteer. Three other nuns answered the bishop's call. Sisters Xaverius Lynch, Xavier Maloney and Bernard Kirwin.

Having obtained the permission of the Bishop of Galway, four cloaked and hooded figures left their convent shortly before 4:00 o'clock on the morning of August 12th to catch the mail coach to Dublin. There were tearful farewells as everyone knew the parting would be forever. Sister Mary Bernard, who was the burser of the Galway convent, was appointed Superior of the group. Dr. Fleming and his boy, Phil Doolan, rode on the outside in the box with the driver. He had promised Mother John, in writing, that if the sisters did not like Newfoundland, he would land them safe back in their own parlour again "without a penny of expense to the house."

When they arrived in Dublin the nuns were quartered in the house of a Mrs. Hughes on Ormond Quay. One morning a young priest was sent there to say mass for them. However, a venerable deacon who got there before him turned the young man away, saying, "Well, my boy, what do you know about nuns?" The priest's name was John Mullock and on a future day, as Fleming's successor to the See of St. John's, he would become their spiritual Superior.

From Dublin the ladies travelled to Waterford. August 28th, in the tiny village of Passage, they boarded the ship *Ariel* as it came down river from Waterford and headed for the Atlantic. They were only a few hours at sea when the group became almost insensible with seasickness. On the third day there was a terrible storm which broke off one of the masts. It lasted three days. The bishop quickly found his sea legs, but the ladies lay in their bunks moaning, too sick to be frightened. Soon after that first storm, they were struck by another that lasted 36 hours, and they were sure every moment would be their last. The sails were torn to pieces and monstrous high waves swept the deck. Sister Magdelene reported: "The vessel heaved so much we could not stand even for a minute. You may be sure there is not a saint in the calendar who was not invoked during this violent storm."

When the *Ariel* finally reached Newfoundland waters, heavy fogs and off-shore winds prevented it from entering the Narrows and the vessel tossed about for three more days and nights in sight of the town. At 6:00 o'clock on the morning of Friday, September 21st, they finally entered the harbour. Before they left the vessel, an address was presented to Dr. Fleming by members of the Newfoundland Parliament. As they all crossed to the dock in a small boat they saw the wharves, banks and hills of the town covered by cheering crowds, so that their "ears were stunned with the noise and cries." Sister Xaverius wrote that

"Protestants, Orangemen and all kinds of people came to welcome us."

They landed at the wharf of James Tobin, opposite Holloway Street, and after being served a cup of tea by Mrs. Tobin in her living quarters above the merchant's premises, they travelled by carriage through cheering crowds to the Bishop's residence on Henry Street hill, where they occupied two rooms and a parlour and began searching for a suitable school. They found it on Duckworth Street between Pilot's Hill and Cochrane Street. The building had been a tavern known as The Rising Sun and the sisters took the name to be a propitious omen. They opened their school on Monday morning, October 21st, and enrolled 450 poor girls as pupils. The Rising Sun tavern became the first school taught by English-speaking nuns in British North America.

Meanwhile, their report on the voyage and reception in St. John's, which the sisters sent to their convent in Ireland, went astray in a Liverpool post office. When months passed without any word from them reaching Galway, they were given up for lost and their vows burned in the sorrowful ceremony of mourning that accompanied the death of a nun. It was six months before the truth was known.

Soon after the school opened, Bishop Fleming went to inspect it. He was appalled to find there was a blacksmith's forge at the back of the building. In order for the horses to reach the forge, they had to go through the hallway of the school. In spite of the year's lease, he determined to move the women immediately to more suitable lodgings. He rented a house from the Church of England rector of St. Thomas's, Archdeacon Wix, in the vicinity of Holloway Street on what became Nunnery Hill. Here the sisters stayed for nine years. When the lease ran out, they moved into a beautiful new convent near the top of Long's Hill. Two years after they moved, the building was destroyed in the Great Fire which leveled St. John's in June of 1846.

Bishop Fleming was away at the time of the fire, so the nuns took it upon themselves to go and live that summer in the barn of his farm at Carpasia on what is now Carpasian Road. (The Presentation Sisters have a novitiate today on the same property). They were five months living in the barn when the bishop returned. He immediately sent them to share the convent of the Mercy Sisters on Military Road. Plans were made for a new mother house and school on Cathedral Square.

Mother Bernard and her band of pioneers found the cold of the Newfoundland climate a severe hardship. Those were the days when there was little heat in any house during the day, except for the kitchen, and none at all during the night. They wrote home to Ireland that the water froze in the rooms, even with a fire and they were obliged to cut the milk for breakfast with a knife from a solid lump. Their breath froze on the bed sheets. The frost was so intense that while mopping the stairs, the water froze to the boards and cloths left to steep became a complete mass of ice. Sister Magdelene wrote of her pupils: "from their appearance you would scarcely think you were teaching in a poor school. No such thing as a barefoot child to be seen here, how great the contrast between them and the poor Irish!" Some of these letters were interrupted in the writing by the ink freezing in the inkwells.

The Rising Sun tavern continued in use as a school until a new schoolhouse opened in 1834. Constructed under the supervision of the bishop, it was close to the residence of the sisters on Nunnery Hill. While most of the pupils were Roman Catholic, it also accepted Protestant girls, which gave Archdeacon Wix grounds for complaint, although he continued to collect his rent from the nuns without a whimper in that regard. Within three years of their arrival in St. John's, the Presentation Sisters had enrolled 600 scholars in their school. From 1836 the four women were paid £100 per year by the government towards expenses.

Bishop Fleming, already ill and worn out from his labours, got a severe shock when he returned to Newfoundland late in 1846 to find St. John's burned to the ground. The shock permanently undermined his health and before he could begin to rebuild the Presentation Convent, he was in his grave beneath the high altar of the cathedral he was building. His successor, John Mullock, laid the cornerstone August 23, 1850, and the sisters took possession July 2, 1853, even though the living quarters were unfinished. They spent the spring and summer of that year sheltering under a canvas roof made of ship's sails.

It is interesting to learn what became of these four Irish women, so dedicated to the service of God and the education of poor girls that they could give up homeland and friends forever, face the hazards of an ocean voyage, and endure hardship and calamity in Newfoundland to establish the first overseas branch of an order founded by a Cork woman, Joanna (Nano) Nagle, in 1775, which afterwards spread throughout the world. They influenced education in a century when few women in Newfoundland had any influence, except as mothers.

Mother Bernard Kirwin was born in Galway's parish of Moineva in 1797. Her parents, James and Ann Kirwin, were influential people of means. She was highly educated in music, needlework and French. She was also trained in business. In 1823 she offered herself as a Postulant with the Presentation Sisters in her home town and was professed in 1826 as Sister Mary Bernard. She served as Superior in St. John's for six years when, under the rules of the order, she had to step down. In September, 1853, she was sent as foundress to Admiral's Cove, Fermuse, where she died February 27, 1857, and was buried beneath the parish church. When the building burned down in 1940, a memorial was placed over her grave. Two attempts to remove her remains to St. John's have been resisted by people of the area, who renamed Admiral's Cove, Port Kirwin in her honour.

Sister Xavier Maloney, born in 1783, was the oldest of the four. She was fifty years of age when she volunteered to go on the Newfoundland venture. In 1853 she went as foundress to Harbour Main. A few years later Sister Xavier was taken ill and had to return to St. John's. She died in 1865 and is buried behind the Mother House on Cathedral Square.

The youngest of the first group of volunteers was 20 year-old Sister Xaverius Lynch, born in 1813. She was sent to Harbour Grace in 1851. The house she founded there was the first branch of the Sisters of the Presentation of the Blessed Virgin Mary in Newfoundland. As Superior she was greatly loved by both the sisters and their pupils. Her service to the community in Harbour Grace stretched over nearly thirty years. She died in the convent she founded and built November 25, 1882, and lies buried in Harbour Grace.

Sister Magdelene O'Shaughnessy was an example of the first being last. While the first to volunteer for the Newfoundland mission, she was the last to die. Born November 12, 1797, and professed in 1823, she was thirty-six-years old when she answered Bishop Fleming's knock on the door of the Galway Covent. When Mother Bernard's term of office expired in 1840, Sister Magdelene became Superior at St. John's. It was under her direction that the convent on Long's Hill was built and she was responsible for the construction of the new school and mother house at Cathedral Square. September 20, 1883, her golden jubilee, was joyously celebrated in St. John's with Bishop Howley writing an operetta for the occasion. It was under Mother Magdelene's direction that the Presentation Sisters opened their first foundations outside St. John's. She died March 2, 1889, at the advanced age of 92 years, fifty-six of them spent labouring in the cause of education in Newfoundland. She was British North America's first nun.

Chapter Fifteen

Misfortune and Death — the Seal Hunt Legacy

The pros and cons of the grim necessity that is known as the annual seal hunt are not for debate here, but they should lead us now and then to take a brief look at the tragic disasters that have befallen what one writer has called "the greatest hunt in the world." The major sealing ship tragedies concern the SS *Greenland* in 1898, the SS *Newfoundland* and SS *Southern Cross* in 1914 and the SS *Viking* in 1931.

First news of the shocking event that became known as *The Greenland Disaster* was nearly a week reaching St. John's, because in 1898 there were no wireless sets on any ships. Marconi's historic experiments were three years in the future. On Monday, March 21st, the SS *Greenland* was picking up seal pelts 70 miles north of the Funk Islands. Enough seals to load the ship had been killed and panned, but the men of another steamer had plundered the catch.

Anxious to make good his loss, Captain George Barbour put all his men out on the ice. The morning was fine and clear as he sailed to the northeast, dropping four watches on the way. After sailing back along the three-mile path to the first swilers, he began taking on pelts until six o'clock when a wind storm, accompanied by blinding snow squalls, suddenly swallowed up the afternoon. The first watch was hastily taken on board, but before the ship could sail to pick up the other sealers she was jammed tight in the closing ice.

As darkness fell the storm grew in intensity. The men stranded on the ice suffered terribly from the intense cold. Few seals had been killed that day so there was little or no fat to make a fire. The abandoned men waited all through the night, but daylight brought no relief. The blizzard continued all day Tuesday. Some of the swilers wandered off in search of their vessel and were never seen again. Others died of exposure where they lay on the ice. The frost and hunger were unremitting. Several sealers fell into holes of water and drowned. It was after four o'clock when the storm began to abate, but by then darkness was falling. All through the second night the stranded men still alive heard the ship's whistle constantly blowing, but there was no way they could walk over the jagged peaks of ice to reach her. They were too exhausted.

Wednesday morning a lead opened in the ice and the vessel was able to get clear and start picking up the sealers. Of the 54 men caught in the storm, only six survivors were found, along with 24 corpses which were stripped naked and packed in ice on the port side of the ship. Saturday evening the SS *Greenland* called in at Bay de Verde and word of the tragedy was flashed by telegraph to St. John's, where thousands lined the waterfront on Sunday afternoon to watch the mournful ship sail in through the fog-shrouded Narrows. The bodies were dug from the ice, wrapped in quilts and taken by horse and sleigh to the Seamen's Home on Duckworth Street, a place that afterwards served for many years as City Hall. Funeral services took place on Tuesday. Forty-eight men had perished.

In a storm that struck Newfoundland on the afternoon and night of March 31, 1914, two disasters took the lives of 253 sealers. The vessel SS *Southern Cross* vanished without a trace in a blizzard that quickly roared out of threatening skies. She was on her way back to St. John's from the Gulf with 17,000 seals on board. In the morning the SS *Portia* passed her heading across St. Mary's Bay towards Cape Race. That was the last that was ever seen of her or any member of her crew.

Around the time the two vessels were passing each other in signs of a gathering storm, the weather on the northeast coast of the island promised a good day. Captain Wesley Kean of the SS *Newfoundland* put his men on the ice with instructions that, should the weather turn bad, they were to spend the night on his father's ship, the SS *Stephano*. With that young Kean sailed almost out of sight.

During the forenoon a group of men from the SS *Newfoundland* who found few seals so far that day on the hunt went aboard the SS *Stephano* for a mug-up. When the weather showed signs of turning bad, Captain Abram Kean put his son's men back on the ice and sailed away to pick up his own men. None dared tell the famous and feared sealing captain that his son's orders were for them to stay on his father's ship. As the sealers made their way in the direction in which their own vessel had vanished, a vicious blizzard suddenly enveloped them and it raged without remission for twenty-four hours. Some men stumbled into holes of freezing water and quickly died. Others fell exhausted on the ice and perished in huddled groups. Some stamped about and sang hymns throughout the night in an effort to keep their circulation going.

Around two o'clock next afternoon it finally stopped snowing, but the drifting made it impossible for anyone to see the ship through the blowing snow. The survivors were forced to spend a second harrowing night fighting the bitter frost and their hunger. Soon after daylight on Thursday rescue came in the form of the SS *Bellaventure*, when a lookout on her thought he spied a patch of seals ahead on the ice. The excitement turned to horror as they drew near and realized the "seals" were the frozen bodies of dead sealers. Of 136 men caught in the blizzard 78 had perished. The men of the SS *Bellaventure* had to hack the corpses from the ice with axes.

As in "the *Greenland* Disaster" of 1898 silent crowds lined the docks of St. John's when survivors and the dead reached port. Bodies were stacked on deck like logs and those wounded by the frost leaned in agony on the rails. Amputations were necessary and many were scarred for life by their ordeal. Some bodies were frozen in praying positions and most of those who died in each other's arms had to be thawed in vats of boiling water in Harvey's shed, before they could be separated. The nearby King George V Institute, erected by Sir Wilfred Grenfell, served as a morgue. The wounded occupied two wards of the General Hospital. The familiar parades of mourners to the churches and cemeteries filled the streets of St. John's. The story of this tragedy is movingly told in Cassie Brown's book, *Death on the Ice*. Seventeen years later the scene was to be repeated.

The SS *Viking* was built at Arendal, Norway, in 1881. From 1904 Bowring Brothers used her continually in the seal fishery. In the spring of 1930 an American film producer, Varick Frissel, who had learned his trade from the great Robert Flaherty, chartered the SS *Ungava* for a semi-documentary film, *Northern Knight*, dealing with the Newfoundland seal hunt. It was the first American feature sound film shot on a foreign location and the first feature length Canadian film. It starred a very handsome young American actor named Charles Starrett who made his film debut that year opposite Carole Lombard in *Fast and Loose*. He was afterwards to star in 130 westerns, more than any other American actor and, for 14 years, from 1937, he was to be among the 10 top moneymaking western stars.

When the picture, retitled *White Thunder* was shown to the studio bosses in New York they felt it lacked an exciting climax. It was decided to have the film company return to St. John's in the spring of 1931 and shoot some additional scenes of icebergs rolling over. To accomplish this a large stock of dynamite was required. The SS *Ungava* was unavailable so her role in the film was assumed by another sealing ship, the SS *Viking*. Charles Starrett's film commitments kept him in Hollywood, but Frissel and the rest of the movie crew sailed from St. John's on board the venerable sealing vessel as she headed north towards the patches.

Sunday, March 15th, the *Viking,* under command of Captain Abram Kean Jr., was steaming off White Bay with her crew of sealers, the movie people, their gear and dynamite filling all available space, when an explosion suddenly tore the ship apart. The scene of carnage and desolation was dreadful, as men and boys with shattered limbs crawled about among the mutilated bodies of their dead companions on the blood stained ice.

It has been said that almost every family in Newfoundland has been touched by some sea tragedy and it was this one that touched my own. Among the dead was an 11-year-old stowaway, Edward Cronan, my first cousin. In those days stowing away on sealing vessels was a favourite pastime among Newfoundland boys. On that fateful voyage, 12 youthful stowaways were taken off before the vessel left Bowrings, and another 9 lads were discovered and removed while she was still in port. However, three escaped detection until the ship was steaming north. The navigator, Captain Will Kennedy, the brother of my uncle-by-marriage, was so badly wounded that he died on the way back to St. John's.

White Thunder was completed in Hollywood, but the title was changed a third time to *The Viking* so as to obtain maximum publicity from the tragedy. Besides its interest to film historians as the first Hollowood sound picture made on a foreign location, it is of estimable value to Newfoundlanders because the movie's introduction contains the only voice-on-film of that famous autocratic humanitarian, Sir Wilfred Grenfell. In it he pays tribute to Frissel and the film crew and vouches for the authenticity of the seal hunting scenes. Another reason for Newfoundlanders to cherish *The Viking* is that the part of the captain in the picture is played by a real life captain, the great Arctic explorer, Bob Bartlett. All known prints of the film disappeared until 1950, when an old shed belonging to Job's firm was being demolished in St. John's to make way for Harbour Drive. A nitrate print was found stored, forgotten, on a shelf. It was carefully transferred to regular film by the Canadian film archives in Ottawa, where it is now preserved as the first feature-length sound film shot in what is today Canada.

The tragic events that befell the *Greenland, Southern Cross, Newfoundland* and *Viking* are just three of numerous seal hunting disasters that fill the pages of Newfoundland history. In 1830 the *True Blue* sank at Petty Harbour Motion on her way home from the hunt and 30 men were lost. Four years later the Carbonear vessel, *Mary,* went down with 24 of her crew. Details of the great hurricane in the spring of 1838 are hard to come by, but it is believed that 14 ships were lost in that storm and about 300 persons perished. It is said "the mournful cry of the starving widow and her mite" was a familiar one throughout the land.

Twenty-one men of Harbour Grace lost their lives in the sinking of the *Margaret* in 1847. Only one man and a boy survived among a crew of 26 when the *John and Maria* went down off Brigus coming home from the seal fishery in 1857. Ten years later, in 1868, 28 deaths resulted from the loss of four boats belonging to the ill-fated *Deerhound*. The *Village Belle* and her crew of 18 men sailed to the ice in 1872 and were never seen again. That same year the loss of the *Huntsman* accounted for 43 deaths. Of the 18 who were rescued only three were not seriously injured. A boiler explosion on board the SS *Tigress* killed 21 of her crew in 1874 and badly wounded others.

Landsmen as well as swilers on board ships have suffered maiming and death while trying to eke out a subsistence by hunting seals. It was in 1867 that 10 women and 2 men died while looking for seals from land off Catalina. In 1892 a calamity known to history as the "Trinity Bay Disaster" claimed the lives of 24 landsmen who perished amidst the ice floes off shore. Rev. P. Carolan sent the following dispatch to St. John's from Trinity Bay, "Woe, woe, unutterable woe, crushes us today. Sobs and lamentations rend the air and corpses are strewn along the shore...victims of Saturday's gale which crushed the bight and swept off the men...who were out in punts seal hunting; some drifted back dead, some dying...." The 20th century is also littered with the scarred and frozen bodies of Newfoundland seal hunters.

Chapter Sixteen

David Bennett — Newfoundland's Sousa

The most remarkable name in 19th century Newfoundland music was that of a man whose career spanned over seventy years of that century — Professor David Bennett. He appears to have been among the most ubiquitous of music masters, for there was probably not a single event of importance in the colony, from the early 1830s to the early 1890s, in which some band to which he belonged did not lend a musical accompaniment. Yet for all that, he is generally neglected when it comes to naming the famous men of Newfoundland's past.

David Bennett is believed to have been born in St. John's where, at an early age, he entered the service of the Royal Newfoundland Company with the ambition to be trained, not as a soldier, but as a musician. This would indicate his family was of modest circumstances and unable to afford private lessons. The lad displayed a wondrous natural ability and a passionate love for music, so that he soon mastered the rudiments. After a few years with the Royal Newfoundland Company Band, he was pronounced by critics of the day to be a first class performer. During his time with the company he was often called upon to perform solo before the principal inhabitants of the town and their guests. In 1836 he played for Governor Prescott and subsequently appeared before every governor from that time until that of Governor Maxse in 1882.

Young Bennett was not content to follow the batons of others. He wanted to lead his own band and the opportunity first presented itself when the Total Abstinence and Benefit Society was formed in 1857. In those days every self-respecting organization had its own band, so Bennett was hired by the T.A. Society as Band Instructor. He was to hold the post for twenty years.

A subsequent appointment that was to take on great

importance with the passage of time was that of Band Master to No. 2 Company, known as the Queen's Own Volunteers. Later the various companies merged into one batallion and Bennett found himself Band Master to the whole force. He remained in the post until the companies were disbanded with the departure of the military from Newfoundland in the early 1870s.

In 1858 St. Bonaventure's College was opened by Bishop Mullock as a seminary for the training of clergy, with the priest who was to become Bishop Carfagnini of Harbour Grace as its President. A few years later, in 1863, Dr. Mullock appointed David Bennett Professor of Music on the staff of the college which included the Hon. Thomas Talbot, Maurice Fenelon, and Dr. Richard Howley. He remained professor of music at St. Bonaventure's for twenty years. The appointment did not stop him from taking the post of teacher with the Star of the Sea Band immediately after that society's formation.

Professor Bennett's various bands gave added distinction to numerous events throughout his long career. His group played before His Royal Highness, Prince Henry of the Netherlands, during his visit to St. John's in 1845 and they played before His Royal Highness, the Prince of Wales (afterwards King Edward VII), when he called at St. John's in 1860.

John Philip Sousa in his heyday was no more busy than David Bennett and his band. He played for the famous fencing of the Basilica grounds and afterwards played for the digging of the foundation. When Bishop Fleming laid the corner stone for his cathedral, Bennett and his boys were there. During some of the celebrated hauls of stone from Signal Hill to the cathedral site his music encouraged the volunteers. When Archbishop Hughes of New York consecrated the place in the presence of other prelates the Bennett band performed, just as it had on the morning the dying Bishop Fleming said the first mass in the uncompleted structure. On that ocasion he also played first violin with the choir. In fact the consecration of the cathedral was a busy time for the professor. His band played at the public breakfast given in the old Orphan Asylum School to honour the New York Archbishop and visiting bishops, and it performed again at a large dinner party given for them by Governor Harvey at Virginia Water. Later he was to play for the first haul of stone for St. Patrick's Church, and he led the College Band at the great bazaar held in Fishermen's Hall to aid St. Patrick's. They also played at the ceremony when the corner stone was blessed, as well as provided music for the consecrations of the new churches at Blackhead, Ferryland and Torbay.

Professor Bennett's own band was made up of members of the bands of such societies as the Mechanics, Total Abstinence, Star of the Sea, Phoenix and Cathedral Fire Brigades, most of which he conducted. His group played for the laying of the foundation stone of the Star of the Sea Hall on Henry Street by Bishop Power, and again for the laying of the foundation stone of the Christian Brothers residence, Mount St. Francis. For twenty-five years they were on hand to render music for the first Mass on Christmas morning in the cathedral. There was no Midnight Mass in those days. On special occasions he played for religious ceremonies in the Presentation and Mercy Convents. He was, himself, always a part of the musical programs which used to be presented in the Episcopal Library. When Bishop Howley's operetta in honour of Mother Magdalene's golden jubilee was presented, he directed the music for the premiere, as well as for a subsequent performance in the presence of Archbishop O'Brien of Halifax.

In 1878 Professor Bennett had the honour of playing at the head of the great parade in St. John's to welcome Bishop George Conroy of Ireland, the first Apostolic Delegate to visit Newfoundland. He arrived on June 27th intending to spend much of the summer in St. John's. Unfortunately, after being in the country only two weeks, he was taken ill and by August 4th he was dead. Bennett had the unexpected bonus of playing for the delegate's funeral mass before the corpse sailed away on the SS *Caspian*.

Besides his services to the Roman Catholic Church David Bennett was endlessly active in the community. His bands played at the various rinks and theatres around town in winter, and in the parks and on the promenades in summer.

The corner stone of the new institution for the confinement of lunatics, to be known as the Lunatic Asylum, was laid at 4:00

107

o'clock on the afternoon of July 27, 1853, by Governor Hamilton and his Lady. It was put in place by three strokes of the mallet, while Professor Bennett's band rendered a rousing version of "The Banks of Newfoundland." The ceremony was followed by dancing in the open air "to the spirited music of the band until the shades of evening."

When the Atlantic cable was dragged ashore from the *Great Eastern* at Hearts Content in 1866, Professor Bennett's band was there to welcome it. The group afterwards played for the "grand fete" held in the Colonial Building to honour the cable's great promoter, Cyrus Field.

The first passenger trip on Sir Robert Reid's new railway line was a grand excursion to Topsail. The train left the little station at Fort William at 9:00 o'clock sharp on the morning of June 29, 1882, accompanied by the Bennett band. When they tired, the professor led the Star of the Sea Band, as well as another unnamed band, in providing musical airs throughout the excursion. Bennett was also Band Master for the Anglican Church Lads' Brigade when the CLB was organized and in need of music instruction.

This remarkable man, who played with the military in the reign of William IV, lived to see the reign of Edward VII. He was active in the music field in Newfoundland throughout the entire 64 years of Queen Victoria's reign. At the time of her death in 1901, he was still giving occasional lessons to pupils on various instruments and seemed to have lost none of the accuracy in imparting musical information which characterized him throughout his life.

Bennett's abilities were passed on to his sons. Three of them, Thomas, Harry and John, played in his band. Thomas and Harry predeceased their father. Thomas was magistrate for the Central District of St. John's. He died in 1872. John was engaged as Musical Instructor to the Terra Nova Constabulary Band by Inspector General McCowen.

In his private life David Bennett was said to be retiring and of an unobtrusive disposition, moved by no praise nor carried away by any acclaim. He was awarded the Medal of Merit of the British Army for general good conduct and his eminent services to the military as a musician. A lover of his art, it is said he practiced it without ostentation. His merit and ability were never questioned throughout the whole of his long life, and when he was almost an octogenarian, his performances on the violin were said to be as perfect as they were half a century before. His sense of criticism was always keen and he was not reluctant to voice it amongst those who played in his bands.

It was said of Bennett that he was a man totally absorbed in his music and without enemies, having endeared himself to all with whom he had come in contact. Unfortunately, the many tokens of the high esteem in which he was held were destroyed when all his wordly possessions were burned in the great fire of 1892, including his music and instruments. He was too old to rewrite his own compositions so they remain lost to us.

In his last years, after the turn of the century, Professor Bennett continued to take a personal interest in the musical events of the city, and there was no public gathering in which music played a part that he did not attend. His mental faculties were unimpaired and physically he was as erect as he had been at fifty. It was only when he recalled some prominent event he had taken part in sixty or more years before that one was reminded of his age.

One of the legacies of Professor Bennett was Charles Hutton, a young man he discovered and set on the highroad to musical immortality in Newfoundland. Although Hutton was to outshine Bennett in the eyes of posterity, no one was to equal him as a Band Master. He can rightly be called the John Philip Sousa of Newfoundland.

In remembering the happy moments and pleasant hours of bygone days, the Newfoundland historian, H.F. Shortis, vividly recalls to mind, in the *Newfoundland Quarterly* for October 1901 "...the many happy hours spent in listening to the music of either the Military, the Bonaventure or the Volunteers Bands, of all of which he [Bennett] was the soul and life." He also recalled "...the pleasant summer evenings spent in the Episcopal Gardens, — on the Parade, or on the Mall, which places were often rendered lively by the dulcet music, presided over and led by — Professor David Bennett."

Chapter Seventeen

Death By Tidal Wave — The Burin Disaster

At 4:32 p.m. on the afternoon of November 18, 1929, I had just been taken from my cot following my afternoon nap in our house at Bay de Verde, when my mother felt the room shake and saw dishes fall from the shelves of the kitchen dresser. She wondered what on earth was happening. That evening at 7:00 o'clock, as supper was being cleared away, there was another tremor which my father surmised to be an earthquake, but such a thing happening in Newfoundland was so rare he dismissed it from his mind.

It was not so easy to dismiss the series of tremors in towns scattered along the foot of the Burin Peninsula as it was on the northern tip of the Avalon. Nineteen-year-old Pat Antle was returning from a shopping errand when he heard the first rumble that afternoon. He thought it was an airplane in the distance, but then the earth began to shake and the noise increased to a deafening roar. People poured out of their houses wondering at the cause. A man who had been in Halifax during the 1917 tragedy that had blown up a section of that city thought it was probably the explosion of a ship loaded with explosives in Burin, seven miles away.

As darkness fell over the peninsula, Antle made his way to a friend's house where a group of eight people started a game of forty-fives. As the dealer was shuffling the cards they felt the house shake. Soon somebody was heard outside, shouting that the community was sinking. Everyone scrambled to windows and doors to see a giant wave about thirty feet high sweeping in over the land. The tidal wave tore boats from their moorings, ripped stages and waterfront sheds from their foundations and flooded the ground floors of many houses along the ocean front.

Pat Antle says of that terrifying minute, "The noise of smashing timbers, the roar of the sea, the movement of thousands of tons of rocks and beach gravel, the screams of horrified people, all blended into one indescribable crescendo."

The first wall of water was followed by a second wave that was not as high, but almost equally devastating. In Lamaline the telephone operator saw what was happening and shouted into her transmitter, "The sea is coming in." Before she could articulate a cry for help, the building was smashed from its foundations and she barely escaped with her life. At Burin, 60 miles along the Peninsula, the telephone operator had no time to give any kind of warning as the wave swept in over the community of 1200 people, drowning ten of them. Following the second tremor in the town of St. Lawrence people noticed that the water drained out of the harbour, which was normally 30 feet deep in places. Sensing what was about to happen they scrambled for high ground.

In fifteen minutes from Lamaline to Burin the tidal waves killed 36 people. Along the 70 miles of coastline about 500 houses and stores were destroyed. One hundred fishing boats were lost as well as 26 schooners. In land-locked harbours such as Burin and St. Lawrence, reached by narrow channels from the sea, the energy compressed between the high walls of rock built up to gigantic proportions. It was reported that at one place the waves gouged a hole 5 feet deep and 10 feet wide.

The first quake, at 4:32 p.m., was of major magnitude with a reading of 7.2 on the Richter scale. The epicenter was about 250 miles southeast of Burin. The tsunami (as the seismic sea waves which follow an earthquake are called in science) were the first in recorded history to damage the east coast of North America.

As the waters began to recede on Monday night the misery of the survivors, and those who set out in dories and small boats to look for people in distress, was accentuated by a howling northeast wind accompanied by a blinding snowstorm. In spite of these conditions there were many acts of heroism. Some men in a dory saw a house floating by half submerged in the water. A kerosene lamp still burned brightly through the dark in an upstairs window. When they broke out the window and climbed inside, they found a baby asleep in a bed completely unharmed. The mother and three older children had been drowned on the first floor.

In Port au Bras six people lost their lives. All boats and waterside premises were gone. Six were drowned in Port au Gaul and nearly a hundred buildings destroyed. Four lives were lost in Taylor's Bay with 15 families homeless and no waterfront property left. Lord's Cove had many of its houses swept out to sea and three persons drowned. The waterfront in Lamaline was left in complete ruins with twelve lives lost. Two died at Kelly's Cove. There was a miracle of sorts in Ship Cove when a house and all its occupants was swept out to sea by one wave and back again on land by another, allowing everyone to escape.

Tragedy was commonplace in the devastated area. One man, 70 years old, lost his wife and four grandchildren. Another, 83 years old, lost his wife and all that he possessed. A 52-year-old, sick with T.B. for seven years and no prospects of working again, lost all his possessions. A man who lost his wife and three children in the disaster was so affected by his personal tragedy that he became badly depressed and had to have the title to his house lodged in trust with Magistrate Hollett in Burin, so that he might not be deprived of his property by any mistake of his own in selling or otherwise.

The Honourable George Bartlett, a prominent merchant and member of the House of Assembly for Burin District, was in his shop when the first tremor was felt. He afterwards likened it to "a tremendous roar and vibration." Everyone rushed outside to see what was happening. The worst that befell the merchant was some goods tumbled from the shelves of his shop. By evening the wind dropped and the moon rose clear and bright. In the calm of nightfall Bartlett went to visit his friends, Captain John Whelan and Inspector Dee, on board the Newfoundland Customs cutter *Daisy* tied up at the government wharf.

They were just finishing a cup of tea and preparing for a game of cards when a sailor burst into the cabin to report that the whole town was sinking. The men rushed on deck to see the cutter floating in over the wharf, while around them were the frightening sounds of water smashing harbour-front stores and dragging houses from their foundations. After five minutes the sea subsided and Bartlett was able to jump to the wharf. He found his shop, a building fifty-five by thirty feet, resting in a meadow 200 feet from its foundation but with supplies intact.

Great damage had been done to the 12 transatlantic cables that ran to and from Europe on the nearby ocean bed. Likewise, telegraph lines between St. John's and the Burin Peninsula were knocked out and in those days there was no road connection. From Monday to Thursday the south coast tragedy was unknown to the rest of the colony. It was not until Thursday morning, when the coastal steamer, *Portia*, called at Burin and discovered the catastrophe that news of it was wirelessed to St. John's. The SS *Meigle* was dispatched from the capital that evening loaded with doctors, nurses, medical supplies and food for the destitute people of the peninsula. Besides their boats, fishing premises and houses, many fishermen also lost their season's catch which had not yet been sold to the local merchants. Replacement of supplies alone would cost millions at a time when the spectre of depression was beginning its decade-long appearance throughout the land.

Those on board the *Meigle* heard many fantastic stories of the heroism of men struggling through swirling waters, smashing out windows and dragging terrified women and children to safety. One man from Port au Bras was attempting to reach his house when it swirled past with his wife and children peering out through a window. They were never again seen alive. In Mortier a young man leaped to a rooftop, saved an elderly woman from a floating house, and in the process ruptured a blood vessel. He had to walk two miles to Burin for medical aid and arrived in a state of shock.

Dorothy Cherry, a young English nurse who operated the dispensary at Lamaline, worked seven straight days without rest tending to the sick and wounded. Alone, she began in Lamaline and worked her way along the shore to Burin, travelling on foot when her horse gave out. On some barren stretches of the highroad she had to wade icy streams where the bridges had been washed out. In addition to other hardships, the weather was bitterly cold and snow fell. When the SS *Meigle* reached Lawn Nurse Cherry was brought on board in a state of near collapse.

A South Coast Disaster Committee was organized in St.

John's and a quarter of a million dollars was raised to aid the survivors, with help coming from all over the world. Without warning, following a series of earth tremors, the ocean had risen up and deluged the land, crushing peoples' homes and carrying away their relatives, friends and possessions for a distance of some seventy miles along the coast. Forty towns and fishing villages, affecting a population of 10,000 people, were involved in grief and disaster. The cost of the damage in dollars was estimated at two million.

Chapter Eighteen

Two Women Who Dared To Be Different

The first two Newfoundland women to make a mark in professions, other than as school teachers or religious, did so in the field of medicine. Both were the daughters of well-to-do merchant families, yet neither was ever a militant suffragette. Margaret Rendell became the first Newfoundland-born registered nurse and Edith Weeks the first native-born female doctor, as well as being the first woman to practice medicine in Newfoundland.

George Thomas Rendell and his brother William emigrated from Devon, England, to St. John's in 1843 and established the firm of W. & G. Rendell on Water Street in 1861. George was a prominent layman in Church of England affairs and through his friendship with Rev. Martin Wood, Rector of St. Thomas', met the clergyman's daughter Lizzie, a sister of Canon T.M. Wood. The couple married and in 1862 Lizzie gave birth to a daughter, Margaret Alexandra. There were several other children in the family but Margaret did not allow them to dominate her. She grew into a tall, thin girl who asserted her independence with such determination it may even have frightened off would-be suitors. By the time she was thirty years old, her marriage prospects were thought to have dimmed to the point where she determined on a career to support herself, even though her father was a man of means.

George Rendell, strange to say, appears to have placed no obstacles in his daughter's way when she advised him of her wish to become a nurse. The head of the school of nursing at Johns Hopkins University in Baltimore was Adelaide Nutting, who, after Clara Barton, was to become possibly the greatest name in American nursing. Miss Adelaide Nutting and her sister Armine had come to St. John's in 1882 to teach at the Church of England Girl's Academy on King's Bridge Road. Minnie was in charge of the school and Addie taught music. Unfortunately, the demand for lessons on the pianoforte from a female teacher by the daughters of society was so meagre that Adelaide was unable to support herself and, at the end of the year, decided to return home to Ottawa. Minnie, who was attracted to a pale young man from Bermuda who shared the table at Mrs. Coen's boarding house on Prescott Street, chanced staying behind. Her gamble paid off and she married William Gosling, who eventually became mayor of St. John's. On his death she donated his library to the city. It became the Gosling Memorial Library.

Adelaide eventually decided to abandon music for nursing. Sir William Osler, a friend of the family, was establishing a school of nursing at Johns Hopkins in Baltimore and Addie graduated with the first class. Osler recognized her great ability and made her his assistant. Later he put her in charge of the Nursing School. While in St. John's the Nutting sisters would have known the Rendells. Adelaide is said to have taught Margaret piano lessons, as she was accomplished at the keyboard. In any case when it came time for Margaret to leave Newfoundland for training as a nurse, instead of following the more normal route to England, as did her later contemporary Mary Southcott, she joined Miss Nutting's classes in Baltimore and graduated from Johns Hopkins in 1897.

After a brief period of gaining practical experience in the United States, Margaret returned to St. John's. Newfoundland nurses up to her time were not only untrained, but most were also illiterate. Medicines in the hospital were identified by different coloured paper wrappers on the bottles because these women were unable to read.

On her return home Margaret Rendell joined the staff of the General Hospital, where she was appointed matron in 1898, taking over from Miss Collins, who came out from England in 1895, to become the first professionally trained nurse to work in Newfoundland. Shortly after her appointment, Margaret Rendell developed a romantic interest in George Shea, a widower who, at forty-seven, was twelve years her senior. He was the son of Sir Edward Dalton Shea, a newspaper publisher, MHA for Ferryland, member and later President of the Legislative Council, and a nephew of Sir Ambrose Shea. George had also served as MHA for Ferryland 1885-1893. He married Nurse Rendell in 1899. It was an age in which a working wife was not tolerated, except among the lower classes, and she was forced to retire from the General Hospital and give up her nursing career. Her husband became the first elected mayor of St. John's two years later, in 1902.

Margaret Rendell Shea continued to find excitement by becoming the first Newfoundland-born woman to drive an automobile. It is reported that chicken, geese and people all scurried out of the way as she came along the road in a cloud of dust, clipping the odd picket from a fence. March 24, 1908, she gave birth to a son, Ambrose, called after his great uncle, a man numbered among the Fathers of Confederation for whom the CN Ferry was named. After a military career in the British and Canadian Armed Forces, Ambrose Shea served as Private Secretary to Hon. Fabian O'Dea and Hon. E. John Harnum when they were Lieutenant Governors of Newfoundland. He died in 1978, the last of the great Shea family.

Margaret Rendell was born in a house on the south side of Duckworth Street, just west of Cochrane Street. In 1879 her father erected a new house, which is still standing, on the east corner of Cochrane Street and Military Road. She lived there with him and afterwards with her husband, who purchased it from his father-in-law's estate. At the time of her son's marriage to Tessa Hutton in 1935 she conveyed the property to Ambrose and moved to the Newfoundland Hotel, where she resided for many years. She died in the Cochrane Street House, May 18, 1949, and is buried in the Rendell plot in the Anglican cemetery on Forest Road.

At the time Margaret Rendell was graduating from Johns Hopkins in 1897, the girl who was to become Newfoundland's first female medical doctor was fifteen years old and living with her parents in Bay Bulls and St. John's. Hamilton Weeks, born in Hamilton, Ontario, was married in St. John's in 1875 to Margaret Weir, a girl born in Glasgow, Scotland.

Hamilton and Margaret Weeks had two children, a son, Albert, and a daughter, Edith. The girl was born at Bay Bulls, April 23, 1882. Her father was Job's agent on the Southern

Shore and one of the leading Newfoundland fish merchants of his day. Weeks' premises at Bay Bulls (afterwards taken over by Gerry Williams and known as the "—boom defence" during World War Two) was one of the largest mercantile establishments in Ferryland District. All that remains today of the once imposing house and shop that stood next to the fish stores, flakes and wharf on the waterfront is a garbage littered foundation.

What first attracted the twenty-year-old daughter of this family of means to seek a career in medicine is unknown. Nothing she ever told her son or daughter has enabled them to speculate. Whatever the reason, Edith Weeks took pre-med with the Faculty of Medicine at Dalhousie University, Halifax, in 1902-03. From there she went to the University of Toronto, where she graduated from Trinity College in 1906 with the degree of Doctor of Medicine and Master of Surgery. December 31, 1906, she registered with the Newfoundland Medical Board and joined the staff of the St. John's General Hospital where she served for the next four years. During that time she lived in her father's town house at 30 Leslie Street.

In 1910 Hamilton Weeks, who was then sixty-two years old, decided to retire and move to the more equitable climate of British Columbia. He sold his business interests in Newfoundland. His son, Bert, and his daughter, Edith, went with their parents. Bert was drowned soon after when a schooner his father bought him went down between the British Columbia mainland and Vancouver Island. Edith resumed the practice of medicine in Vancouver, where she must have been one of the first female doctors in British Columbia.

In 1912 she met and married Henry Hooper, an Australian working for the Canadian firm of Makin's. Their first encounter had been on the platform of a railway station in Montreal when Hooper spied what he thought was the most beautiful woman he had ever seen. He spoke to her, took a room at the boarding house where she was staying, and their romance blossomed.

When World War One broke out, Henry Hooper wanted to join the Australian forces, so the couple embarked on the long sea voyage across the Pacific to Sydney. It was such a trying

118

experience that Edith, who feared the sea which had taken her brother, spent the rest of her life in Australia, a country for which she had an undisguised dislike, rather than face the ocean journey back to Canada.

Dr. Edith Weeks Hooper gave birth to a son, James, March 28, 1917, and to a daughter, Edith, February 2, 1919. As these children grew, their demands on her time and attention by 1922 were such that she resigned her position as a doctor with the Queen Victoria Home for Consumptives, Thirlman, New South Wales, and retired from a practice she had in Hunter Street, Sydney. When World War Two seriously depleted the ranks of doctors on the Australian home front, she returned to medical work and was a doctor with the Mental Health Department from 1942 until 1945, at which time she retired permanently.

Henry Hooper died December 26, 1948. In the years following his return to Sydney from Canada he became a prosperous commission agent. The Great Depression nearly bankrupted him. Edith, who had always been used to plenty in the family homes at Bay Bulls and St. John's, deeply resented this setback in her husband's financial fortunes and, after having been socially prominent, withdrew into her private world, sharing few of her emotions and little of her past life even with her own family. In her last days in Australia her mind began to wander back to her childhood, and she sometimes imaged herself in the sitting room of the old house at Bay Bulls, greeting visitors from Witless Bay and Petty Harbour. She died in Sydney June 10, 1964 at the age of 82 years.

People in Bay Bulls still remember Dr. Weeks as a young woman in her late twenties, coming out from St. John's for the occasional weekend at her parents' house. When she did, she would get young Matt Coady (who died in 1978) to tackle the horse, Flying Cloud, a former Prince Edward Island tandem racehorse, to the carriage and take her to Witless Bay where she would see patients in Luce Mullowney's front room. He was a brother of Lady Gertrude Cashin. The Mullowney house burned to the ground in 1977 while being restored. One lady presently living in Bay Bulls, Mrs. Agatha Joy, recalls Dr. Weeks treating her for an eye infection when she was a small girl. Mrs. Joy still has in her possession a wash basin, jug and soap dish belonging to Mr. and Mrs. Hamilton Weeks and acquired by her mother when the family moved to British Columbia.

October 26, 1978, the Health Science Complex in St. John's, containing the new General Hospital and Memorial University School of Medicine, was officially opened. In a special ceremony the previous evening, two framed pictures were presented to the new hospital. They were of Margaret Rendell in her graduation uniform, taken at Johns Hopkins, Baltimore, in 1897, and of Edith Weeks in her graduation gown, taken at the University of Toronto in 1906. It had taken Joyce Nevitt, author of *White Caps and Black Bands*, and me, two years of painstaking research to track down the photographs which we presented to the General Hospital. As things turned out, they were the only pictures known to be in existence of Newfoundland's first native-born registered nurse and first female medical doctor. Ambrose Shea had died several months prior to the presentation of his mother's picture, but Dr. James Hooper, Superintendent of Mater Misericordiae Hospital, Waratah, New South Wales, travelled all the way from Australia to St. John's to be present for the presentation of his mother's photograph. His sister, Edith, had visited her mother's homeland a few months previously.

Chapter Nineteen

The U.S. Occupation of Newfoundland in 1941

During the War of 1812 between the United States and Britain, Newfoundland was faced with the possibility of an American invasion and forts around the shores of the island prepared for an attack which never materialized. One hundred and twenty-nine years later in a global war, U.S. forces in their thousands landed in Newfoundland, many from a former German ocean liner, and their occupation of the country was to last nineteen years without the firing of a shot in anger.

September 30, 1940, United States representatives travelled to Newfoundland to inspect Argentia as a probable U.S. naval base site. Two days later the group arrived in St. John's and took a look at Pleasantville, then a green valley generally known as Ross's Grove on the north shore of Quidi Vidi Lake. In November another party visited Stephenville to consider that community as a possible airfield site.

What precipitated this activity was the desire of the American government to set up an outer ring of defense bases in the British West Indies, Bermuda and Newfoundland. The British Government's asking price for these bases was 50 obsolete U.S. Navy destroyers of the flush-deck type, lying at anchor for years in various dockyards along the Atlantic Coast. Britain desperately needed these old vessels to protect her convoys from enemy submarines. In order to get the deal approved, President Roosevelt assured Congress that the risk of the transfer to American neutrality was far less than any danger of attack for lack of an outer ring of eastern defences.

Since Newfoundland's status as a Dominion was suspended at the time, the suggestion was made that the rights required by the United States should be given without consideration to the colony. The only Newfoundlanders consulted were the three who served on the Commission of Government and they were told to make secret and tactful enquiries to see how the idea would be received by their countrymen. Sir Edward Emerson, Commissioner for Justice and Defence, suggested that the retention of American extraterritorial rights be made the basis of peacetime negotiation between the restored Government of Newfoundland and the United States. The British Commissioners rejected the Emerson stipulation and sent an unreserved acquiescence to the War Cabinet in London.

The United States troopship, *Edmund B. Alexander* (the former German luxury liner SS *Amerika*), arrived off St. John's, January 25, 1941. On board the 21,000-ton vessel were 1000 United States soldiers who were the first Americans to serve on foreign soil in World War Two. Their leader was Colonel Maurice Welty. It was not until four days later that the weather cleared enough for the huge army transport to enter harbour about one hour after sunrise of the 29th, when two tugs and two coastal steamers nudged her to a berth on the southside. A dense fog soon obliterated the town and the ship's band could be heard playing "Hail, Hail, the Gang's All Here" to lift the spirits of the G.I.s trying to peer through the icy mists.

The troops lived on board what was known as "the swankiest floating barracks afloat" while Colonel Welty established his headquarters in the former residence of Sir Richard Squires, 44 Rennie's Mill Road. April 14th a lease was signed with Carpasian Park Ltd. for fifteen acres of land between Pine Bud Avenue, Carpasian Road and Long Pond Road for the erection of a tent community to house the American servicemen. There were boardwalks over the muddy ground, outdoor latrines and camp kitchens. The soldiers' tents were heated by wood stoves. It was a miserable existence for anyone used to the comforts of home.

May 5, 1941, construction work was begun on an installation on the North Shore of Quidi Vidi to be known as Fort Pepperrell. It was named for Sir William Pepperell, a relation of the wife of Sir Leonard Outerbridge of St. John's. Pepperrell led the land forces at the capture of Louisburg, Nova Scotia, in 1745, and had the distinction of being the first native-born American to be created a baronet. It seemed a safe choice.

On May 20th, soldiers were moved from the ship to Camp Alexander, as the Carpasian Park property was known. While they settled in for the summer, construction forged ahead at Pleasantville. This work was a blessing for the country where tens of thousands of people were still on relief as a result of the depression. That summer of 1941 there were virtually no unemployed in Newfoundland, as Fort McAndrew at Argentia and Harmon Field at Stephenville were also under construction.

There was a controversy over the wages to be paid to Newfoundlanders. The Americans were ready to accept the principle of wage parity, with local workers being paid on much the same scale as their American and Canadian counterparts. But the Commission of Government felt this would have a disastrous effect on the Newfoundland economy, making it impossible for local firms to find employees and thereby closing down essential industries. The Americans were persuaded to pay the Newfoundland workers at a much lower scale than they had intended. A fourth United States base was begun at Goose Bay and that brought employment to the Labrador coast. Prosperity was everywhere.

The money which the United States government poured into Newfoundland in building the bases at St. John's, Argentia, Stephenville and Goose Bay put the bankrupt colony back on its financial feet, and ended the horrors of the depression. November 24, 1941, the G.I.s at Camp Alexander folded their tents like the Arabs and moved into Fort Pepperrell where their comfortable two-storey, flat-roofed barracks were of wood with asbestos shingles on the outside. Colonel Welty moved his headquarters from Rennie's Mill Road to the new base in February, 1942.

Fort Pepperrell was originally an army base. After World War Two it was switched to Air Force control. The effect which the many thousands of American servicemen who were stationed at the base over the years had on such a close-knit community as St. John's may be too big for sociologists to measure, but there can be little doubt that in the long run they changed the lives of much of the population forever. It has been estimated that 10,000 U.S. servicemen married Newfoundland girls and they and their children are today scattered in possibly every state in the Union.

April 14, 1958, was a day of grave misgivings in St. John's when there was official confirmation of the long circulated rumours that Fort Pepperrell, or Pepperrell Air Force Base, as it was then known, was to be phased out. Everyone was making gloomy predictions that the closing would be a disaster for the economy. Like mourners at a wake, thousands poured through the gates to witness the final Armed Forces Day celebrations on May 17th, realizing it would be the last such event. It took nearly two more years for the phase-out to be completed, as other bases in Newfoundland and Greenland were being shut down at the same time. May 15, 1960, the United States Army Transportation Command Arctic, then in charge of the operation, closed the gates of Fort Pepperrell for the last time.

When the extraterritorial rights in Newfoundland were awarded to the United States Governmment, the lease was for 99-years, and at the time it seemed like forever. Nobody dreamed it would mean just over eighteen years. The development of modern, inter-continental weapons and technological advances in warfare had made Fort Pepperrell and the others in Newfoundland obsolete. The bases at St. John's, Argentia and Stephenville had cost the United States Government 100 million 1941 dollars and, by agreement, they reverted to the Canadian Federal and Newfoundland Provincial Governments for $1.00, but there was a wrangle over ownership between the two governments. Fort Pepperrell was divided at the Virginia River, with the Federal Government taking most of the buildings west of the river and the Provincial Government taking most of the buildings east of the river.

In a special ceremony in August 1961, the Stars and Stripes was lowered for the last time at Fort Pepperrell and the Canadian flag was run up. In 1966 Harmon Field was closed as a military base. Argentia remains in United States Navy control with a simple "caretaker" status. Goose Bay also has a very small American presence left.

It was another of Newfoundland's many misfortunes not to

have had its own government at the time the bases deal was made with Britain. Part of the bargain might have been closer economic ties with America and a settlement to the century-old Newfoundland fishery problem. Churchill said to Sir Edward Emerson after the signing of the agreement, "I can readily appreciate the feelings...you told me might arise that Newfoundland was being asked to give up much of what she holds of value....Without this agreement it would be impossible to say what would be the effect on the prosecution of the war and the whole future of the world...."

Whether or not, as Mr. Churchill seemed to be suggesting, the Newfoundland base deal had done much to save the world from the ravages of Adolph Hitler, it certainly saved Newfoundland from the poverty of the '30s. At the peak of U.S. construction in the country, 19,000 people were employed and, in spite of the low wage of 30¢ an hour for general labour, it was an era which saw the place prosper as never before in its history. At the same time, the demand for newsprint had the Grand Falls and Corner Brook mills working at capacity. Orders for Bell Island and Buchans ore rose and the fledgling fresh-frozen fish industry flourished.

Several times the war came close to the shores of Newfoundland, but President Roosevelt's outer ring of defence bases never had to defend the United States from direct enemy assault. Four Bell Island natives working in a waterfront shed were killed one bright summer's day during the war, when a German U-boat sank four ships as they lay in the shelter of the island loading iron ore. They were the only persons killed on what is now Canadian soil by enemy action in World War Two. Another submarine fired two torpedoes at an old coastal steamer in the Narrows at St. John's hoping to block the harbour entrance. One blew up without harm when it struck the rocks below Fort Amherst. The other lodged in one of the anti-submarine nets without exploding and was defused.

Whatever the social impact of the American occupation of Newfoundland in 1941, there can be little doubt that the prosperity it brought drove the Commission of Government and the people farther apart. Newfoundlanders began to look forward to the end of the war when they hoped the fundamental privileges of political democracy would be restored.

Chapter Twenty

The U-Boat Sinking of the SS *Caribou*

Most travellers visiting Port-Aux-Basques, Newfoundland, on their way to or from Nova Scotia, hurry on or off the CN ferry, without every seeing the grim memorial at the foot of a bleak hill erected to an earlier Port-Aux-Basques-North Sydney ferry sunk by enemy action in World War Two.

When Sir Robert Reid pushed the Newfoundland Railway to the west coast of Newfoundland in 1898, a ferry service was put in operation to link the island to Nova Scotia where passengers could board trains for points in Canada and the United States. This service began with the famous SS *Bruce*. It was carried on by the *Lintrose, Kyle* and others. Work on the gulf boats was pretty much a family affair among people of the south west coast, and fathers, sons, brothers and cousins often served on the same vessel.

Undoubtedly the gulf ferry whose name will live longest in memory was SS *Caribou*. The New Waterway Shipbuilding Company of Schiedam, Holland, was awarded the contract to construct this sleek, modern vessel and she was launched June 9, 1925. Just over four months later she reached St. John's for the first time October 22, 1925, under command of Captain L. Stevenson. He had previously served as Captain of both the *Lintrose* and *Kyle*. His great knowledge of conditions on the gulf was employed in preparing the design of the *Caribou* and she was built especially for easy manoeuvring in the heavy ice which frequently blocks the waterway in spring.

The new ship was well appointed in her dining rooms and smoking saloons and her cabins were fully equipped and very comfortable. After a period of inspection at St. John's, the vessel began her tri-weekly service, crossing the ninety-six miles of water in about eight hours. It was a leisurely voyage on a smooth ship that was noted for the courtesy and concern of her officers and crew. Nothing was too much trouble for the welfare of a passenger. In the 1920s and '30s there were no passenger airplanes to and from Newfoundland, and a gulf ferry was a busy ship. The *Caribou* service went well for fourteen years. Then, in 1939, Hitler invaded Poland and World War Two broke out.

At first the war did not affect shipping in Newfoundland waters, but as the holocaust in Europe dragged on U-boat activity in the North Atlantic increased until the island found itself in the target zone. The Captain of the *Caribou* and Newfoundland Railway officials were strong in their opinion that all wartime sailings across the gulf should be in daylight. However, the Canadian Naval authorities insisted on night crossings. Departures from Sydney and Port-Aux-Basques were on a regular schedule with a set time for sailing that was available to anyone who inquired, friend or foe. During her annual survey in September 1942, the ship was fitted with emergency life rafts in addition to her life boats.

At seven o'clock on the evening of October 13, 1942, the SS *Caribou* sailed from Sydney on her regular night crossing carrying a crew of forty-six. There were seventy-three civilian passengers and 118 servicemen for a total of 237 persons on board. There was accommodation for 284 and boats and life belts for 300 people. The ship was escorted by a Canadian Bangor Class minesweeper, HMCS *Grandmere*. The escort was to stay with the ferry for the whole of the passage. The military personnel were embarked first and it was sometime later that the civilian passengers went on board. They consisted of the usual collection of children, students, housewives, businessman and commercial travellers. As the ship moved away from the Cape Breton shore the night was fine with some stars showing. A slight swell accompanied a light wind. On board ship everything was completely blacked out and passengers were warned not to show any open lights on deck. If the officers and crew were nervous of these night crossings they did not show it. The stewardess, Bride Fitzpatrick, went about her duties in the cabins with a cheerful smile. By midnight most passengers were in their bunks asleep and the decks were almost deserted. The engines droned on in their routine way.

At twenty minutes to three in the morning, when the *Caribou* was forty miles south-west of her destination, the routine was shattered by an explosion. A torpedo from a German U-boat had torn apart the starboard side. At the moment the ship was struck, HMCS *Grandmere* was on her starboard quarter. The escort sighted the submarine on the surface ahead and to starboard. She attempted to ram the enemy but the U-boat dived when *Grandmere* was still 150 yards off. The escort dropped a pattern of depth charges, but the counterattack was inaccurate and the enemy got away. She dropped two more patterns in the neighbourhood, but was unable to locate the submarine by Asdic.

Although the sudden crash-dive caused chaos on board the 500 ton U-69, Captain Graf and his crew congratulated themselves on avoiding being rammed, and on their quick evasive action in getting away from the depth charges. The U-boat, known to her crew as the "Laughing Cow", had entered the Gulf of St. Lawrence at the beginning of October. On the ninth she sank the small British steamer SS *Carolus* of 2537 tons. Since there was no other prey in sight, she was on her way out to open sea when she chanced upon the gulf ferry.

Meanwhile, on board the *Caribou*, there was much confusion. Passengers awakened by the loud explosion had little idea of what caused it. However, the ship began to list badly almost at once and it was obvious something serious had occurred. Many were still dressing and trying to get into their life jackets before going out on deck when the lights went out without warning. There was much shouting and people were running up and down the companionways trying to find their way in the dark. When they reached the boat deck, they discovered that the main deck on the starboard side was already under water. Two of the life-boats had been destroyed by the explosion, but a third was successfully launched. Because of the heavy list only one boat got away from the port side. The emergency life-rafts installed the previous month were now of the utmost importance if many were to be saved.

On the bridge, Captain Benjamin Tavernor steered the sinking ship at the surfaced submarine, but the U-boat submerged. Many people were still standing on deck trying to free the life-rafts when the *Caribou* sank beneath them. It was estimated that five minutes after the sound of the explosion the ship was gone.

There were large numbers of people floundering around in the cold, dark waters of the gulf and some of the life-rafts were badly overcrowded. One broke apart, throwing everybody into the sea. All the women and children who could be found were placed on another raft. One airman, F/0 Jack O'Brien of Amherst, Nova Scotia, went floating by with two small infants tucked inside his Air Force greatcoat, one on each side of his chest.

It was obvious that the rafts in the area when the ship went down could not possibly hold all the people who were thrashing about in the water. Some of the better swimmers and those in life-jackets contented themselves with clinging to the ropes on the sides. Everyone was soaked to the skin and numb with cold, but there was a generally high spirit of optimism. The first light of dawn was greeted by cheering and an attempt was made to get a sing-song going. Everyone seemed to join in, but it was not easy for the survivors to keep their spirits up during the next three hours as aircraft flew close, but failed to spot them in the freshening wind which increased the swell.

One report stated that the U-boat surfaced in the midst of a group of survivors, smashed a lifeboat and upset several rafts before sighting the escort vessel and diving. There were complaints that rescue operations were delayed nearly five hours, because the escort was employed in an unsuccessful effort to track down the submarine.

At six o'clock in the morning news of the tragedy was received at the Newfoundland Railway headquarters in St. John's. Within an hour a small fleet of six boats was sent out from Port-Aux-Basques to pick up any survivors they could find, while a special train was made ready to carry them to St. John's. At 8:30 the *Grandmere* came upon a group of three rafts filled with people. The crew offered them their own warm clothing and coffee laced with a stimulant. 103 survivors were pulled from the water, but two died on board the *Grandmere*.

Around 8:30 she was relieved by HMCS *Reindeer* and HMCS *Elk* so that she could carry the survivors to Sydney. They were landed at twenty minutes to five in the afternoon, many in need of medical care. Those who wanted to were flown to Newfoundland by Trans Canada Airlines, which had begun operations in and out of the city.

When the rescue was complete, it was found that 137 lives had been lost, including Captain Ben Tavernor and two sons who were serving officers on the ship. Of those who survived, thirty were seriously injured. Eight were kept in hospital. The only surviving ship's officer was Tom Fleming, who afterwards served as purser on another gulf ferry, the *William Carson*, that sank on a passenger run. Just as the gangway was being removed from the *Caribou* in Sydney before she sailed on her last voyage, a man jumped aboard. His name was not on the passenger manifest as it had already been completed and sent ashore. The fellow's name and destination were unlisted. While in the water, shortly after the ship went down, Tom Fleming spotted Charlie Moores, a railway employee, and told him about the unlisted passenger so the information could be recorded if he didn't survive.

One Corner Brook businessman numbered among the survivors was William J. Lundrigan, who afterwards founded one of the greatest industrial empires in Newfoundland history. Mr. Lundrigan gave up his cabin berth to allow some women to have somewhere to sleep and was bedded down in the lounge when the torpedo struck. He managed to find his way into one of the few lifeboats that were successfully launched. It is certain he could not have done this had he retained his cabin berth. Lundrigan and the other survivors praised the officers and crew for the way in which they averted panic in the face of certain death.

With the help of J.V. Ryan, Assistant General Manager of the Newfoundland Railway at the time, the Railway Employees' Welfare Association raised funds for the construction of a memorial at Port-Aux-Basques. Thirty-one crew members were lost, including stewardess Bride Fitzpatrick. They left twenty-one widows and fifty-one orphans, mostly in the Port-Aux-

Basques area. Captain Benjamin Tavernor and his two sons were commemorated in the name of the coastal vessel, SS *Tavernor*, which went into service in 1962.

Naval Authorities later admitted there were at least three German submarines in Newfoundland waters at the time of the sinking of the *Caribou*. The vessel sailed on her crossings under Naval orders, with a Naval escort, and regularly transported Allied Military Personnel, so she was a legitimate target. It is said that as far as the ship's officers were concerned the question was not, "Will she be sunk?" but, "When will she be sunk?" The slogan "Remember the *Caribou*" was to inspire patriotic zeal in Newfoundlanders for the remainder of World War Two.

The following official German report ends the wartime tragedy: "The U-69 commanded by Captain-Lieutenant Ulrich Graf, was sunk on February 17, 1943, by HMS. *Viscount*. Captain Graf was lost with his boat."

Chapter Twenty-One

Alcock and Brown — First to Fly the Atlantic Non-Stop

If John Alcock and Arthur Whitten Brown had been Americans, there is no doubt that their names would be as well-known to the world today as Charles Lindberg. Long ago cinema audiences would probably have seen Clark Gable as John Alcock and Robert Taylor as Arthur Whitten Brown in an M.G.M. movie spectacular of the first non-stop flight across the Atlantic. However, the two heroes were Englishmen and their feat is celebrated mainly in a statue of the two airmen which puzzles travellers outside Heathrow Airport in London. There is also a monument in Ireland and three indifferent memorials in St. John's.

The great adventure began in 1919 when Lord Northcliffe in his influential newspaper, the London *Daily Mail*, offered a prize of ten thousand pounds for the first non-stop flight across the Atlantic in a British-built, British-manned, heavier-than-air machine. This eliminated Americans, Frenchmen and Germans from the competition. In the spring of 1919 airmen began arriving in St. John's to compete for Lord Northcliffe's award of fifty thousand dollars, a considerable sum of money at the time.

Soon there were three groups vying for the prize. In St. John's there was Harry Hawker and Lt. Commander J. McKenzie-Grieve with a Sopwith biplane, named *Atlantic*, and F.P. Raynham and Commander Morgan in a Martinsyde biplane, called by a name compounded from the first three letters of each of their names, *Raymor*. At Harbour Grace a rather more sophisticated group under Rear Admiral Mark Kerr had assembled a third aircraft. May 13, 1919, well after the others had begun their preparations, the two St. John's groups were joined by a pair of late-comers, John Alcock and Arthur Whitten Brown. Their crated Vickers Vimy bomber was unloaded from a ship in St. John's harbour and taken to Pleasantville, while the two airmen, who shared rooms with the others in the competition at the Cochrane Hotel, drove to Mount Pearl in search of an airfield. There was none to be had. It seemed as if the other two groups had acquired the only level ground around St. John's. Hawker and Grieve were using Glendennings Farm at Mount Pearl (now the agricultural research station) and Raynham and Morgan were using a field on the north shore of Quid Vidi Lake (now a sports field).

St. John's, at the time, was playing host to several correspondents from abroad who had come to Newfoundland to cover the departure from Trepassey of the United States NC flying boats that were island hopping across the Atlantic. Only one of four flying boats actually made it to Lisbon via the Azores. U.S. destroyers were stationed every fifty miles along the route of the air fleet to flash beacons and send up star shells as guides. There were originally five planes but the NC2 never left New York. The NC5 became lost in the fog over Newfoundland and, after flying about for some hours in a fruitless search for Trepassey, landed in St. John's harbour where the British flyers were among the crowds she attracted to the waterfront. After take off she steered an erratic course through the Narrows, but was soon a total loss. The NC1 and NC3 also crash-landed in the sea. The NC4 reached Lisbon, May 17, 1919, to be the first aircraft to fly the Atlantic.

Even though the Americans had taken every precaution the navy could devise to get their sea planes across the ocean, the threat of the venture caused Hawker and Grieve, as well as Raynham and Morgan, to abandon caution and risk everything in an attempt to win for Great Britain the honour of completing the first trans-Atlantic flight. As soon as they got word the NC4 had reached the Azores, Hawker and Grieve decided they would try and beat the Americans to Europe, in spite of the fact that their preparations were not complete and flying conditions over the ocean were unfavourable.

Their attempt to be the first to fly the Atlantic, which would also be the first attempt to do so non-stop, was begun at Glendennings Farm, Mount Pearl, May 18, 1919, at twenty-five minutes past one in the afternoon. A historic marker on the grounds of the government Demonstration Farm on Brookfield Road stands near the site today.

In their Sopwith biplane, *Atlantic*, Harry Hawker of Australia and McKenzie Grieve of England took off on what they pretended to Raynham and Morgan was a test flight under a full load. The plane lumbered westward into the sky, rose in the air and flew back over the city at one thousand feet. Beyond the Narrows the undercarriage was released into the sea to lighten the load. It was later recovered by a fisherman off Cape St. Mary's and returned to St. John's.

The biplane travelled at a speed of 125 miles per hour and carried enough fuel for thirty hours. Fourteen hours later, when they were only seven hundred miles from the Irish coast, the flyers were forced down into the sea by mechanical difficulties. They were rescued by the Danish tramp steamer, *Mary*, but since the vessel had no wireless they were given up for lost until the ship docked in Thurso, Scotland, on May 25th.

As soon as Raynham and Morgan heard that Hawker and Grieve had dropped their undercarriage they knew the race was on to be the first across. They hurried to their Martinsyde, the *Raymor*, at Quidi Vidi, but the choice of that field was their undoing. The runway was not long enough for a good run by a plane laden with fuel and the valley was laced with crosswinds. Around four-thirty in the afternoon, two hours after the departure of their competitors, the two flyers taxied down the three hundred yards of meadow and rose twenty feet into the air accompanied by the cheers of thousands. A few moments after take-off a crosswind caught the biplane and it dipped down, so that its wheels struck the ground and broke off. Fifty yards from take-off it crashed. Morgan was seriously wounded by flying glass. Both attempts of May 18, 1919, had ended in failure. Morgan renamed his plane *Chimera* and, after repairs, attempted a second flight across the Atlantic on July 17th with a new navigator, but a crosswind again caused him to crash and he packed up and left for England by ship. By then it didn't much matter because Alcock and Brown had already made history.

May 18th, while their competitors were attempting the

Atlantic crossing, Alcock and Brown were driving up the Southern Shore as far as Ferryland in search of a suitable flying field. On their return journey a passing motorist shouted at them that Hawker and Grieve were gone, and that Raynham and Morgan had crashed. The problem of their finding a runway was solved when Charles Lester, who had carted their plane from the dock to Pleasantville where it was assembled, offered the airmen his field on the Higher Levels. It was found that by adding four smaller fields five hundred yards of fairly up-hill level ground could be obtained, so thirty labourers were set to work blasting and levelling the terrain.

While this work was going on, Commander Kerr's Handley-Page was seen flying over St. John's making test flights from Harbour Grace. Kerr determined to get away as soon as possible but he was overly cautious. Alcock and Brown settled on June 13th, as they considered thirteen to be their lucky number. However, things were not ready on time and it was 3:30 on the morning of the fourteenth before they left their rooms at the Cochrane Hotel for the field to get their aircraft ready for take-off. A black cat sauntered across the nose of the plane and they considered this a good omen. As morning wore on the tanks were filled with 870 gallons of gasoline and forty gallons of oil. With them in the cockpits were sandwiches, chocolate, malted milk, two thermos flasks of coffee and three hundred private letters in a mail bag. Because of the high winds that day, many people thought the attempt was cancelled so there were few sightseers.

Alcock opened the engines all out, turned the Vickers-Vimy into the westerly wind and headed up the slope. Take-off was at 12:58 in the afternoon. The plane vanished beneath the hill and it was assumed she had crashed, but a few moments later she reappeared, climbing steadily and gaining speed as she flew eastwards over the city and out through the Narrows. Sixteen hours and twenty-eight minutes later, the flyers landed in Ireland to become the first to cross the Atlantic non-stop. The story of what happened in those sixteen hours is one of courage and great heroism in the face of enormous odds to accomplish a feat many, at the time, considered to be impossible.

Soon after leaving St. John's behind they flew into a bank of fog, and for seven hours saw neither sea nor sky. A mishap in the fog almost brought their venture to a close. The air-speed indicator failed to register and bad bumps prevented Alcock from keeping the course. The craft went into a spin, twirling rapidly downward from four thousand feet. They emerged almost on top of the water at a very dangerous angle. A quick glimpse at the horizon enabled Alcock to regain control as the plane's wheels skimmed the white caps.

Later they were lashed by snow, hail and sleet for five continuous hours. When that passed, they found themselves in the grip of a strong sou'wester. At one point Brown noticed that the fuel overflow gauge was obscured by clotted snow. It was imperative that the pilot be able to read the gauge to guard against carburetor trouble, as it indicated whether or not the supply of fuel to the engines was correct. The gauge was fixed on one of the centre section struts and Brown had to reach it by climbing out of the cockpit, and kneeling on the fuselage, while holding a strut to keep his balance. A war wound had crippled one of his legs and this was giving him severe pain in the cramped cockpit. The violent rush of biting, icy wind pushed him backward, and it was only with the utmost courage that he was able to reach the gauge and clear the snow from the glass.

By 6:20 next morning the top and sides of the plane were completely covered by a crusting of frozen sleet. It imbedded itself in the hinges of the ailerons and jammed them, so that for about an hour the aircraft had little if any lateral control. Around eight o'clock in the morning, when they started to nose downwards from eleven thousand to one thousand feet, the starboard engine began to pop ominously, as if backfiring through one of its carburetors, but Alcock was able to keep the machine on a slow glide by throttling back. They stayed in cloud all the way down and there was a danger of sudden immersion in the ocean. At five hundred feet they saw beneath them the dull grey sea. For sixteen hours the pilot's hands and feet had not left the controls. At 8:15 a.m., on June 15th, barely visible through the mist, they spotted two tiny specks of land. They crossed the Irish coast ten minutes later and landed in a bog at Clifden,

Galway, at 8:40 a.m., sixteen hours and twenty-eight minutes after taking off from St. John's. They had mistaken the green bog for a pasture and the plane had come to a halt nose down in the turf. "Where are you from?" an Irishman asked. "America," they replied to polite laughter.

Fame and honours awaited the two men as well as the *Daily Mail* prize of ten thousand pounds. Huge crowds greeted them everywhere their trains stopped from Galway to Euston. They reached London still wearing the flying clothes in which they had crossed the Atlantic. Winston Churchill presented the *Daily Mail* prize at a luncheon in the Savoy Hotel and the king conferred knighthoods on both airmen. Wherever they went they were lionized by an adoring public that was to forget they ever existed ten years later in the international hysteria that greeted Charles Lindbergh's solo flight. Be that as it may, nobody can take from Alcock and Brown the honour of being the first across the Atlantic non-stop. Sad to say, Sir John Alcock died in a flying accident near Paris just six months later, in December, 1919. Sir Arthur Whitten Brown gave up flying for his first love, engineering, and died in 1948. The history-making Vickers-Vimy today hangs in the Science Museum, South Kensington, London. Monuments mark the start and finish of the flight on Lester's Field in St. John's and on Derrygimla Bog in Ireland.

Chapter 1

This 24-foot high statue of the explorer Gaspar Corte Real was made in his Lisbon studio by the prominent sculptor Martins Correira and presented to the people of Newfoundland by Portuguese fishing interests to mark 450 years of fishing in Newfoundland waters. (Newfoundland Department of Tourism)

Chapter 2

The cannon gateposts in front of Sts. Peter and Paul Church and the Mercy Convent in Bay Bulls are a legacy of the French invasions of the community. The large cannon are said to be English and the smaller ones French. The four saints atop the cannon are thought to have been salvaged from a shipwreck and donated by Sir Michael Cashin. (Newfoundland Provincial Archives)

Chapter 3

*This painting of the loss of the **Anglo Saxon** at Clam Cove, near Cape Race, April 27, 1863, owes more to the artist's imagination than it does to fact, but it still conveys some of the horror of the most tragic shipwreck recorded in Newfoundland waters.* (Mariners Museum, *Newport News*, Va.)

Chapter 4

The popular Victorian artist, Sir Edwin Landseer, painted the less well-known black and white Newfoundland dog featured in Barrie's play **Peter Pan**, *calling the work "A distinguished member of the humane society." It proved such a favourite, the particular breed was legitimized as the Landseer Newfoundland.* (National Gallery, London)

Chapter 5

*This drawing, thought to be the architect's concept, was called "the new cathedral at St. John's, Newfoundland" when it appeared in the **Illustrated London News**, June 23, 1849. The spire, the crowning glory of Scott's masterpiece, has yet to be constructed.* (Public Archives of Canada)

Chapter 6

*While no artist has portrayed Ann Harvey's attempt to rescue survivors from the wreck of the **Dispatch**, July 12, 1838, it was probably not unlike this dramatic recreation of Grace Darling's exploit ten years later.* (Grace Darling Museum, Bamburgh)

Chapter 7

Captain George Cartwright, after whom the community of Cartwright is named, settled on the Labrador coast in 1770 and lived there 16 years before his debtors forced him to return to England. (Rischgitz Art Studios)

Chapter 8

Peter Easton, who made Newfoundland his base of operations in 1610, was typical of 17th century pirate captains who plundered shipping of all nations and generally amassed great wealth. (After Johnson, History of the Pyrates, *1724)*

Chapter 9

Two soldiers stand guard outside Fort William, at the east end of Military Road, in this drawing by Oldfield about 30 years after the attempted mutiny of April 25, 1800. It was here that a late night party for Colonel Skinner foiled the mutineers plans. Signal Hill is above the shed left with the Narrows on the right. (St. John's City Hall)

Chapter 10

The St. John's produce market shared the ground floor of the old court house with cells for prisoners awaiting trial on the top storey which was entered from Duckworth Street. The post office occupied the middle floor. The murderers of such people as Dennis Summers and Elfrida Pike would have faced trial here had they been caught. (Public Archives of Canada)

Chapter 11

The legend on this painting says "Sir Humphrey Gilbert, knight, drowned in the discovery of Virginia. Anno 1584." After claiming Newfoundland in the name of Queen Elizabeth 1, August 5, 1583, and thereby founding the greatest empire the world has ever known, Sir Humphrey drowned in an autumn gale on the voyage home. (Commander Walter Raleigh Gilbert)

Chapter 12

*The **Great Eastern** in the harbour at Heart's Content after landing the first permanently successful trans-Atlantic cable, July 27, 1866. Six times larger than any ship then afloat, it was to be her fate never to put to sea again after the return voyage.* (Newfoundland Historical Society)

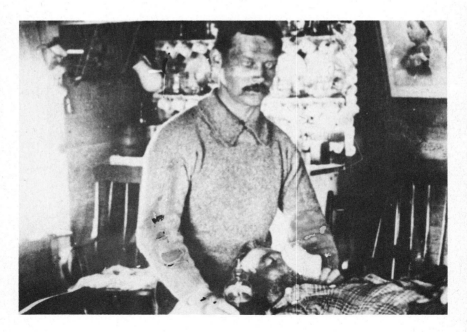

Chapter 13

Dr. Wilfred Grenfell prepares for an operation in the kitchen of a Labrador home in his early years on the coast by administering anaesthetic to a patient lying on the table, while Queen Victoria faces away. The marks on Grenfell's sleeves are damage to the negative. (International Grenfell Association)

Chapter 14

Mother Bernard Kerwin, foundress and first superior of the oldest order of nuns in English Canada, in what is the earliest known photograph believed taken in Newfoundland. She died in 1857 and lies buried at Port Kirwin near Fermeuse. (Presentation Convent Archives)

Chapter 15

*The SS **Viking** at the icefields in a scene from **The Viking**, the first feature film shot in Canada and Hollywood's first foreign location sound feature. When she blew up and sank, March 15, 1931, producer Varick Frissel was among the 27 who died. (Sterling Film Co. Ltd.)*

Chapter 16

Truly the John Philip Sousa of Newfoundland, Professor David Bennett and his many bands played for every important event in St. John's for over half a century. All of the band music which he composed was lost in the Great Fire of 1892. (Centre for Newfoundland Studies, MUN)

Chapter 17

It took just 15 minutes for a tidal wave on the Burin Peninsula in 1929 to drown 36 persons, sink 100 fishing craft and schooners and destroy 500 homes and stores such as this house being towed back to land. (Newfoundland Historical Society)

Chapter 18

*Margaret Rendell Shea, the first Newfoundland-born woman to become a
registered nurse, graduated from Johns Hopkins University, Baltimore,
Maryland in 1897. The following year she became matron of the St. John's
General Hospital.* (Johns Hopkins University Archives)

*Edith Weeks Hooper, the first native-born Newfoundlander to become a
medical doctor, as well as the first woman to practice medicine in
Newfoundland, graduated from the University of Toronto in 1906 and joined
the staff of the St. John's General Hospital. Born at Bay Bulls, she died in
Australia.* (Dr. James Hooper, Sydney, NSW)

Chapter 19

*Soldiers from the troopship **Edmund B. Alexander** lived in Camp Alexander on Carpasian Road from May until November 1941 while Fort Pepperell was being completed. The tent-lined roadway looks south along what is now Sycamore Street with the Basilica towers in the background.* (Leslie Sims, Newport News, Va.)

Chapter 20

John Alcock and Arthur Whitten Brown prepare their Vickers-Vimy bi-plane for take-off at Lester's Fid in St. John's, June 14, 1919. This first successful non-stop flight across the Atlantic to Ireland brought them money, honours and fleeting fame that was eclipsed by Lindbergh's solo flight eight years later. (St. John's City Hall)

Chapter 21

*The ill-fated passenger ferry SS **Caribou** sailed from North Sydney to Port aux Basques on the night of October 13, 1942. Early next morning, while most on board were asleep, a torpedo from a German U-boat sent her to the bottom, bringing the war in Europe to the shores of North America.* (Newfoundland Historical Society)